WHO'S AFRAID OF VIRGINIA WOOLF?

Edward Albee was born in 1928. He has written and directed some of the greatest plays in contemporary theatre, and three of his plays, *A Delicate Balance*, *Seascape* and *Three Tall Women* have received Pulitzer prizes. *Who's Afraid of Virginia Woolf?* won the New York Drama Critics' Circle Award for Best Play.

ALSO BY EDWARD ALBEE

A Delicate Balance

Seascape

Three Tall Women

The Zoo Story

The Death of Bessie Smith

The Sandbox

The American Dream

Tiny Alice

All Over

Listening

The Lady from Dubuque

The Man Who Had Three Arms

Finding the Sun

Fragments

Marriage Play

The Lorca Play

EDWARD ALBEE

Who's Afraid of Virginia Woolf?

VINTAGE BOOKS
London

Published by Vintage 2001

25

Copyright © Edward Albee 1962

Edward Albee has asserted his right under the Copyright, Designs
and Patents Act 1988 to be identified as the author of this work

First published in Great Britain by Jonathan Cape 1964

Vintage
Random House, 20 Vauxhall Bridge Road,
London SW1V 2SA

www.vintage-classics.info

Addresses for companies within The Random House Group Limited
can be found at: www.randomhouse.co.uk/offices.htm

The Random House Group Limited Reg. No. 954009

A CIP catalogue record for this book
is available from the British Library

ISBN 9780099285694

Penguin Random House is committed to a sustainable future for
our business, our readers and our planet. This book is made from
Forest Stewardship Council® certified paper.

Printed and bound in Great Britain by Clays Ltd, Elcograf S.p.A.

FOR RICHARD BARR AND
CLINTON WILDER

CONTENTS

CHARACTERS

MARTHA, *a large, boisterous woman, 52, looking somewhat younger. Ample, but not fleshy*
GEORGE, *her husband, 46. Thin; hair going grey*
HONEY, *26, a petite blonde girl, rather plain*
NICK, *30, her husband. Blond, well-put-together, good-looking*

The scene is the living-room of a house on the campus of a small New England college

Who's Afraid of Virginia Woolf? was first performed at the Billy Rose Theater, New York City, on 13 October 1962 with the following cast:

MARTHA	*Uta Hagen*
GEORGE	*Arthur Hill*
NICK	*George Grizzard*
HONEY	*Melinda Dillon*

Directed by ALAN SCHNEIDER

ACT ONE

FUN AND GAMES

Set in darkness. Crash against front door. MARTHA's *laughter heard. Front door opens, lights are switched on.* MARTHA *enters, followed by* GEORGE.

MARTHA: *Jesus* . . .

GEORGE: . . . Shhhhhhh. . . .

MARTHA: . . . H. Christ . . .

GEORGE: For God's sake, Martha, it's two o'clock in the. . .

MARTHA: Oh, George!

GEORGE: Well, I'm *sorry,* but. . .

MARTHA: What a cluck! What a cluck you are.

GEORGE: It's late, you know? Late.

MARTHA [*looks about the room. Imitates Bette Davis*]: What a dump. Hey, what's that from? 'What a dump!'

GEORGE: How would I know what. . .

MARTHA: Aw, come on! What's it from? *You* know . . .

GEORGE: . . . Martha . . .

MARTHA: WHAT'S IT FROM, FOR CHRIST'S SAKE?

GEORGE [*wearily*]: What's what from?

MARTHA: I just told you; I just did it. 'What a dump!' Hunh? What's that from?

GEORGE: I haven't the faintest idea what . . .

MARTHA: Dumbbell! It's from some goddamn Bette Davis picture . . . some goddamn Warner Brothers epic. . . .

GEORGE: *I* can't remember all the pictures that . . .

MARTHA: Nobody's asking you to remember every single goddamn Warner Brothers epic . . . just one! One single little epic! Bette Davis gets peritonitis in the end . . . she's got this big black fright wig she wears all through the picture and she gets peritonitis, and she's married to Joseph Cotten or something. . . .

GEORGE: . . . Some*body* . . .

MARTHA: . . . some*body* . . . and she wants to go to Chicago all the time, 'cause she's in love with that actor with the scar. . . . But she gets sick, and she sits down in front of her dressing-table. . . .

GEORGE: What actor? What scar?

MARTHA: *I* can't remember his name, for God's sake. What's the name of the *picture*? I want to know what the name of the *picture* is. She sits down in front of her dressing-table . . . and she's got this peritonitis . . . and she tries to put her lipstick on, but she can't . . . and she gets it all over her face . . . but she decides to go to Chicago anyway, and . . .

GEORGE: *Chicago!* It's called *Chicago.*

MARTHA: Hunh? What . . . what is?

GEORGE: The picture . . . it's called *Chicago.* . . .

MARTHA: Good grief! Don't you know *anything*? *Chicago* was a thirties musical, starring little Miss Alice *Faye.* Don't you know *anything*?

GEORGE: Well, that was probably before my *time,* but . . .

MARTHA: Can it! Just cut that out! This picture . . . Bette Davis comes home from a hard day at the grocery store. . . .

GEORGE: She works in a grocery store?

MARTHA: She's a housewife; she buys things . . . and she comes home with the groceries, and she walks into the modest living-room of the modest cottage modest Joseph Cotten has set her up in. . . .

GEORGE: Are they married?

MARTHA [*impatiently*]: Yes. They're married. To each other. Cluck! And she comes in, and she looks around, and she puts her groceries down, and she says, 'What a dump!'

GEORGE [*pause*]: Oh.

MARTHA [*pause*]: She's discontent.

GEORGE [*pause*]: Oh.

MARTHA [*pause*]: Well, what's the name of the picture?

GEORGE: I really don't know, Martha. . . .

MARTHA: Well, think!

GEORGE: I'm tired, dear . . . it's late . . . and besides . . .

MARTHA: I don't know what you're so tired about . . . you haven't *done* anything all day; you didn't have any classes, or anything. . . .

GEORGE: Well, I'm tired. . . . If your father didn't set up these goddamn Saturday night orgies all the time. . . .

MARTHA: Well, that's too bad about you, George. . . .

GEORGE [*grumbling*]: Well, that's how it is, anyway.

MARTHA: You didn't *do* anything; you never *do* anything; you never *mix*. You just sit around and *talk*.

GEORGE: What do you want me to do? Do you want me to act like you? Do you want me to go around all night *braying* at everybody, the way you do?

MARTHA [*braying*]: I DON'T BRAY!

GEORGE [*softly*]: All right . . . you don't bray.

MARTHA [*hurt*]: I do not *bray*.

GEORGE: All right. I said you didn't bray.

MARTHA [*pouting*]: Make me a drink.

GEORGE: What?

MARTHA [*still softly*]: I said, make me a drink.

GEORGE [*moving to the portable bar*]: Well, I don't suppose a nightcap'd kill either one of us. . . .

MARTHA: A nightcap! Are you kidding? We've got guests.

GEORGE [*disbelieving*]: We've got what?

MARTHA: Guests. GUESTS.

GEORGE: GUESTS!

MARTHA: Yes . . . guests . . . people. . . . We've got guests coming over.

GEORGE: When?

MARTHA: NOW!

GEORGE: Good Lord, Martha . . . do you know what time it
. . . *Who's* coming over?

MARTHA: What's-their-name.

GEORGE: Who?

MARTHA: WHAT'S-THEIR-NAME!

GEORGE: Who what's-their-name?

MARTHA: I don't know what their name is, George. . . . You
met them tonight . . . they're new . . . he's in the math
department, or something. . . .

GEORGE: Who . . . who are these people?

MARTHA: You met them tonight, George.

GEORGE: I don't remember meeting anyone tonight. . . .

MARTHA: Well you did. . . . Will you give me my drink,
please. . . . He's in the math department . . . about thirty,
blond, and . . .

GEORGE: . . . and good-looking. . . .

MARTHA: Yes . . . and good-looking. . . .

GEORGE: It figures.

MARTHA: . . . and his wife's a mousey little type, without any
hips, or anything.

GEORGE [*vaguely*]: Oh.

MARTHA: You remember them now?

GEORGE: Yes, I guess so, Martha. . . . But why in God's name
are they coming over here now?

MARTHA [*in a so-there voice*]: Because Daddy said we should
be nice to them, that's why.

GEORGE [*defeated*]: Oh, Lord.

MARTHA: May I have my drink, please? Daddy said we
should be nice to them. Thank you.

GEORGE: But why now? It's after two o'clock in the morning,
and . . .

MARTHA: Because Daddy said we should be nice to them!

GEORGE: Yes. But I'm sure your father didn't mean we were
supposed to stay up all *night* with these people. I mean, we
could have them over some Sunday or something. . . .

MARTHA: Well, never mind. . . . Besides, it *is* Sunday. Very early Sunday.

GEORGE: I mean . . . it's ridiculous. . . .

MARTHA: Well, it's *done!*

GEORGE [*resigned and exasperated*]: All right. Well . . . where are they? If we've got guests, where are they?

MARTHA: They'll be here soon.

GEORGE: What did they do . . . go home and get some sleep first, or something?

MARTHA: They'll *be* here!

GEORGE: I wish you'd *tell* me about something sometime. . . . I wish you'd stop *springing* things on me all the time.

MARTHA: I don't *spring* things on you all the time.

GEORGE: Yes, you do . . . you really do . . . you're always *springing* things on me.

MARTHA [*friendly-patronizing*]: Oh, George!

GEORGE: Always.

MARTHA: Poor Georgie-Porgie, put-upon pie! [*As he sulks*] Awwwwww . . . what are you doing? Are you sulking? Hunh? Let me see . . . are you sulking? Is that what you're doing?

GEORGE [*very quietly*]: Never mind, Martha. . . .

MARTHA: AWWWWWWWWWW!

GEORGE: Just don't bother yourself. . . .

MARTHA: AWWWWWWWWWW! [*No reaction.*] Hey! [*No reaction.*] HEY!

[GEORGE *looks at her, put-upon.*]

Hey. [*She sings.*]

Who's afraid of Virginia Woolf,
Virginia Woolf,
Virginia Woolf . . .

Ha, ha, ha, HA! [*No reaction.*] What's the matter . . . didn't you think that was funny? Hunh? [*Defiantly.*] I thought it was a scream . . . a real scream. You didn't like it, hunh?

GEORGE: It was all right, Martha. . . .

MARTHA: You laughed your head off when you heard it at the party.

GEORGE: I smiled. I didn't laugh my head off . . . I smiled, you know? . . . it was all right.

MARTHA [*gazing into her drink*]: You laughed your goddamn head off.

GEORGE: It was all right. . . .

MARTHA [*ugly*]: It was a scream!

GEORGE [*patiently*]: It was very funny; yes.

MARTHA [*after a moment's consideration*]: You make me puke!

GEORGE: What?

MARTHA: Uh . . . you make me puke!

GEORGE [*thinks about it . . . then . . .*]: That wasn't a very nice thing to say, Martha.

MARTHA: That wasn't *what*?

GEORGE: . . . a very nice thing to say.

MARTHA: I like your anger. I think that's what I like about you most . . . your anger. You're such a . . . such a simp! You don't even have the . . . the what? . . .

GEORGE: . . . guts? . . .

MARTHA: PHRASEMAKER! [*Pause . . . then they both laugh.*] Hey, put some more ice in my drink, will you? You never put any ice in my drink. Why is that, hunh?

GEORGE: [*takes her drink*]: I always put ice in your drink. You eat it, that's all. It's that habit you have . . . chewing your ice cubes . . . like a cocker spaniel. You'll crack your big teeth.

MARTHA: THEY'RE MY BIG TEETH!

GEORGE: Some of them . . . some of them.

MARTHA: I've got more teeth than you've got.

GEORGE: Two more.

MARTHA: Well, two more's a lot more.

GEORGE: I suppose it is. I suppose it's pretty remarkable . . . considering how old you are.

MARTHA: YOU CUT THAT OUT! [*Pause*] You're not so young yourself.

GEORGE [*with boyish pleasure . . . a chant*]: I'm six years younger than you are. . . . I always have been and I always will be.

MARTHA [*glumly*]: Well . . . you're going bald.

GEORGE: So are you. [*Pause . . . they both laugh.*] Hello, honey.

MARTHA: Hello. C'mon over here and give your mommy a big sloppy kiss.

GEORGE: . . . oh, now . . .

MARTHA: I WANT A BIG SLOPPY KISS!

GEORGE [*preoccupied*]: I don't *want* to kiss you, Martha. Where *are* these people? Where are these *people* you invited over?

MARTHA: They stayed on to talk to Daddy. . . . They'll be here. . . . *Why* don't you want to kiss me?

GEORGE [*too matter-of-fact*]: Well, dear, if I kissed you I'd get all excited . . . I'd get beside myself, and I'd take you, by force, right here on the living-room rug, and then our little guests would walk in, and . . . well, just think what your father would say about *that*.

MARTHA: You pig!

GEORGE [*haughtily*]: Oink! Oink!

MARTHA: Ha, ha, ha, HA! Make me another drink . . . lover.

GEORGE [*taking her glass*]: My God, you can swill it down, can't you?

MARTHA [*imitating a child*]: I'm firsty.

GEORGE: Jesus!

MARTHA [*swinging around*]: Look, sweetheart, I can drink you under any goddamn table you want . . . so don't worry about me!

GEORGE: Martha, I gave you the prize years ago. . . . There isn't an abomination award going that you . . .

MARTHA: I swear . . . if you existed I'd divorce you. . . .

GEORGE: Well, just stay on your feet, that's all. . . . These people are your guests, you know, and . . .

MARTHA: I can't even see you . . . I haven't been able to see you for years. . . .

GEORGE: . . . if you pass out, or throw up, or something . . .

MARTHA: . . . I mean, you're a blank, a cipher. . . .

GEORGE: . . . and try to keep your clothes on, too. There aren't many more sickening sights than you with a couple of drinks in you and your skirt up over your head, you know. . . .

MARTHA: . . . a zero. . . .

GEORGE: . . . your *heads,* I should say. . . .

  [*The front door-bell chimes.*]

MARTHA: Party! Party!

GEORGE [*murderously*]: I'm really looking forward to this, Martha. . . .

MARTHA [*same*]: Go answer the door.

GEORGE [*not moving*]: You answer it.

MARTHA: Get to that door, you.

  [*He does not move.*]

  I'll fix you, you . . .

GEORGE [*fake-spits*]: . . . to you. . . .

  [*Door chime again.*]

MARTHA [*shouting . . . to the door*]: C'MON IN! [*To* GEORGE, *between her teeth.*] I said, get over there!

GEORGE [*moves a little towards the door, smiling slightly*]: All right, love . . . whatever love wants. [*Stops.*] Just don't start on the bit, that's all.

MARTHA: The bit? The bit? What kind of language is that? What are you talking about?

GEORGE: The bit. Just don't start in on the bit.

MARTHA: You imitating one of your students, for God's sake? What are you trying to do? WHAT BIT?

GEORGE: Just don't start in on the bit about the kid, that's all.

MARTHA: What do you take me for?

GEORGE: Much too much.

MARTHA [*really angered*]: Yeah? Well, I'll start in on the kid if I want to.

GEORGE: Just leave the kid out of this.

MARTHA [*threatening*]: He's mine as much as he is yours. I'll talk about him if I want to.

GEORGE: I'd advise against it, Martha.

MARTHA: Well, good for you. [*Knock.*] C'mon in. Get over there and open the door!

GEORGE: You've been advised.

MARTHA: Yeah . . . sure. Get over there!

GEORGE [*moving towards the door*]: All right, love . . . whatever love wants. Isn't it nice the way some people have manners, though, even in this day and age? Isn't it nice that some people won't just come breaking into other people's houses even if they *do* hear some sub-human monster yowling at 'em from inside . . . ?

MARTHA: SCREW YOU!

[*Simultaneously with* MARTHA's *last remark,* GEORGE *flings open the front door.* HONEY *and* NICK *are framed in the entrance. There is a brief silence, then . . .*]

GEORGE: [*ostensibly a pleased recognition of* HONEY *and* NICK, *but really satisfaction at having* MARTHA's *explosion overheard*]: Ahhhhhhhhh!

MARTHA [*a little too loud . . . to cover*]: HI! Hi, there . . . c'mon in!

HONEY and NICK [*ad lib*]: Hello, here we are . . . hi . . . [*etc.*]

GEORGE [*very matter-of-factly*]: You must be our little guests.

MARTHA: Ha, ha, ha, HA! Just ignore old sour-puss over there. C'mon in, kids . . . give your coats and stuff to sour-puss.

NICK [*without expression*]: Well, now, perhaps we shouldn't have come. . . .

HONEY: Yes . . . it *is* late, and . . .

MARTHA: Late! Are you kidding? Throw your stuff down anywhere and c'mon in.

GEORGE [*vaguely . . . walking away*]: Anywhere . . . furniture,
   floor . . . doesn't make any difference around this place.

NICK [*to* HONEY]: I told you we shouldn't have come.

MARTHA [*stentorian*]: I said c'mon in! Now c'mon!

HONEY [*giggling a little as she and* NICK *advance*]: Oh,
   dear.

GEORGE [*imitating* HONEY's *giggle*]: Hee, hee, hee, hee.

MARTHA [*swinging on* GEORGE]: Look, muckmouth . . . you
   cut that out!

GEORGE [*innocence and hurt*]: Martha! [*To* HONEY *and*
   NICK] Martha's a devil with language; she really is.

MARTHA: Hey, *kids* . . . sit down.

HONEY [*as she sits*]: Oh, isn't this lovely!

NICK [*perfunctorily*]: Yes indeed . . . very handsome.

MARTHA: Well, thanks.

NICK [*indicating the abstract painting*]: Who . . . who did
   the . . . ?

MARTHA: That? Oh, that's by . . .

GEORGE: . . . some Greek with a moustache Martha attacked
   one night in . . .

HONEY [*to save the situation*]: Oh, ho, ho, ho, HO.

NICK: It's got a . . . a . . .

GEORGE: A quiet intensity?

NICK: Well, no . . . a . . .

GEORGE: Oh. [*Pause*] Well, then, a certain noisy relaxed
   quality, maybe?

NICK [*knows what* GEORGE *is doing, but stays grimly, coolly
   polite*]: No. What I meant was . . .

GEORGE: How about . . . uh . . . a quietly noisy relaxed
   intensity.

HONEY: Dear! You're being joshed.

NICK [*cold*]: I'm aware of that.
      [*A brief, awkward silence.*]

GEORGE [*truly*]: I *am* sorry.
      [NICK *nods condescending forgiveness.*]

GEORGE: What it is, actually, is it's a pictorial representation of the order of Martha's mind.

MARTHA: Ha, ha, ha, HA! Make the kids a drink, George. What do you want, kids? What do you want to drink, hunh?

NICK: Honey? What would you like?

HONEY: I don't know, dear . . . A little brandy, maybe. 'Never mix – never worry.' [She giggles.]

GEORGE: Brandy? Just brandy? Simple; simple. [Moves to the portable bar.] What about you . . . uh . . .

NICK: Bourbon on the rocks, if you don't mind.

GEORGE [as he makes the drinks]: Mind? No, I don't mind. I don't think I mind. Martha? Rubbing alcohol for you?

MARTHA: Sure. 'Never mix – never worry.'

GEORGE: Martha's tastes in liquor have come down . . . simplified over the years . . . crystallized. Back when I was courting Martha – well, I don't know if that's exactly the right word for it – but back when I was courting Martha . . .

MARTHA [cheerfully]: Screw, sweetie!

GEORGE [returning with HONEY's and NICK's drinks]: At any rate, back when I was courting Martha, she'd order the damnedest things! You wouldn't believe it! We'd go into a bar . . . you know, a bar . . . a whisky, beer, and bourbon bar . . . and what she'd do would be, she'd screw up her face, think real hard, and come up with . . . brandy Alexanders, crème de cacao frappés, gimlets, flaming punch-bowls . . . seven-layer liqueur things.

MARTHA: They were good . . . I liked them.

GEORGE: Real lady-like little drinkies.

MARTHA: Hey, where's my rubbing alcohol?

GEORGE [returning to the portable bar]: But the years have brought to Martha a sense of essentials . . . the knowledge that cream is for coffee, lime juice for pies . . . and alcohol [Brings MARTHA her drink.] pure and simple . . . here you are, angel . . . for the pure and simple. [Raises his glass.] For the mind's blind eye, the heart's ease, and the liver's craw. Down the hatch, all.

MARTHA [*to them all*]: Cheers, dears. [*They all drink.*] You have a poetic nature, George ... a Dylan Thomas-y quality that gets me right where I live.

GEORGE: Vulgar girl! With guests here!

MARTHA: Ha, ha, ha, HA! [*To* HONEY *and* NICK] Hey; hey! [*Sings, conducts with her drink in her hand,* HONEY *joins in towards the end.*]

> Who's afraid of Virginia Woolf,
> Virginia Woolf,
> Virginia Woolf,
> Who's afraid of Virginia Woolf ...

[MARTHA *and* HONEY *laugh*; NICK *smiles.*]

HONEY: Oh, wasn't that funny? That was so funny....

NICK [*snapping to*]: Yes ... yes, it was.

MARTHA: I thought I'd bust a gut; I really did. . . . I really thought I'd bust a gut laughing. George didn't like it. . . . George didn't think it was funny at all.

GEORGE: Lord, Martha, do we have to go through this again?

MARTHA: I'm trying to shame you into a sense of humour, angel, that's all.

GEORGE [*over-patiently, to* HONEY *and* NICK]: Martha didn't think I laughed loud enough. Martha thinks that unless ... as she demurely puts it ... that unless you 'bust a gut' you aren't amused. You know? Unless you carry on like a hyena you aren't having any fun.

HONEY: Well, I certainly had fun ... it was a *wonderful* party.

NICK [*attempting enthusiasm*]: Yes ... it certainly was.

HONEY [*to* MARTHA]: And your father! Oh! He is so marvellous!

NICK [*as above*]: Yes ... yes, he is.

HONEY: Oh, I tell you.

MARTHA [*genuinely proud*]: He's quite a guy, isn't he? Quite
   a guy.

GEORGE [*at* NICK]: And you'd better believe it!

HONEY [*admonishing* GEORGE]: Ohhhhhhhhh! He's a
   wonderful man.

GEORGE: I'm not trying to tear him down. He's a god, we all
   know that.

MARTHA: You lay off my father!

GEORGE: Yes, love. [*To* NICK] All I mean is . . . when you've
   had as many of these faculty parties as I have . . .

NICK [*killing the attempted rapport*]: I rather appreciated it.
   I mean, aside from enjoying it, I appreciated it. You know,
   when you're new at a place. . . . [GEORGE *eyes him
   suspiciously.*] Meeting everyone, getting introduced
   around . . . getting to know some of the men. . . . When I
   was teaching in Kansas . . .

HONEY: You won't believe it, but we had to make our way
   all by *ourselves* . . . isn't that right, dear?

NICK: Yes, it is. . . . We . . .

HONEY: . . . We had to make our own way. . . . I had to go
   up to wives . . . in the library, or at the supermarket . . . and
   say, 'Hello, I'm new here . . . you must be Mrs So-and-so,
   Doctor So-and-so's wife.' It really wasn't very nice at all.

MARTHA: Well, *Daddy* knows how to run things.

NICK [*not enough enthusiasm*]: He's a remarkable man.

MARTHA: You bet your sweet life.

GEORGE [*to* NICK . . . a *confidence, but not whispered*]: Let
   me tell you a secret, baby. There are easier things in the
   world, if you happen to be teaching at a university, there
   are easier things than being married to the daughter of the
   president of that university. There are easier things in this
   world.

MARTHA [*loud . . . to no one in particular*]: It *should* be an
   extraordinary opportunity . . . for *some* men it would be
   the chance of a lifetime!

GEORGE [*to* NICK . . . *a solemn wink*]: There are, believe me, easier things in this world.

NICK: Well, I can understand how it might make for some . . . awkwardness, perhaps . . . conceivably, but . . .

MARTHA: *Some* men would give their right arm for the chance!

GEORGE [*quietly*]: Alas, Martha, in reality it works out that the sacrifice is usually of a somewhat more private portion of the anatomy.

MARTHA [*a snarl of dismissal and contempt*]: NYYYAAA-HHHH!

HONEY [*rising quickly*]: I wonder if you could show me where the . . . [*Her voice trails off.*]

GEORGE [*to* MARTHA, *indicating* HONEY]: Martha . . .

NICK [*to* HONEY]: Are you all right?

HONEY: Of course, dear. I want to . . . put some powder on my nose.

GEORGE [*as* MARTHA *is not getting up*]: Martha, won't you show her where we keep the . . . euphemism?

MARTHA: Huh? What? Oh! Sure! [*Rises.*] I'm sorry, c'mon. I want to show you the house.

HONEY: I think I'd like to . . .

MARTHA: . . . wash up? Sure . . . c'mon with me. [*Takes* HONEY *by the arm. To the men*] You two do some men talk for a while.

HONEY [*to* NICK]: We'll be back, dear.

MARTHA [*to* GEORGE]: Honestly, George, you burn me up!

GEORGE [*happily*]: All right.

MARTHA: You really do, George.

GEORGE: O.K. Martha . . . O.K. Just . . . trot along.

MARTHA: You really do.

GEORGE: Just don't shoot your mouth off . . . about . . . you-know-what.

MARTHA [*surprisingly vehement*]: I'll talk about any goddamn thing I want to, George!

GEORGE: O.K. O.K. Vanish.

MARTHA: Any goddamn thing I want to! [*Practically dragging* HONEY *out with her*] C'mon. . . .

GEORGE: Vanish. [*The women have gone.*] So? What'll it be?

NICK: Oh, I don't know . . . I'll stick to bourbon, I guess.

GEORGE [*takes* NICK's *glass, goes to portable bar*]: That what you were drinking over at Parnassus?

NICK: Over at . . . ?

GEORGE: Parnassus.

NICK: I don't understand. . . .

GEORGE: Skip it. [*Hands him his drink.*] One bourbon.

NICK: Thanks.

GEORGE: It's just a private joke between li'l ol' Martha and me. [*They sit.*] So? [*Pause*] So . . . you're in the Math Department, eh?

NICK: No . . . uh, no.

GEORGE: Martha said you were. I think that's what she said. [*Not too friendly*] What made you decide to be a teacher?

NICK: Oh . . . well, the same things that . . . uh . . . motivated you, I imagine.

GEORGE: What were they?

NICK [*formal*]: Pardon?

GEORGE: I said, what were they? What were the things that motivated me?

NICK [*laughing uneasily*]: Well . . . I'm sure I don't know.

GEORGE: You just finished saying that the things that motivated you were the same things that motivated me.

NICK [*with a little pique*]: I said I *imagined* they were.

GEORGE [*offhand*]: Did you? [*Pause*] Well. . . . [*Pause*] You like it here?

NICK [*looking about the room*]: Yes . . . it's . . . it's fine.

GEORGE: I mean the University.

NICK: Oh. . . . I thought you meant . . .

GEORGE: Yes . . . I can see you did. [*Pause*] I meant the University.

NICK: Well, I . . . I like it . . . fine. [*As* GEORGE *just stares at him*] Just fine. [*Same*] You . . . you've been here quite a long time, haven't you?

GEORGE [*absently, as if he had not heard*]: What? Oh . . . yes. Ever since I married . . . uh, What's-her-name . . . uh, Martha. Even before that. [*Pause*] For ever. [*To himself*] Dashed hopes, and good intentions. Good, better, best, bested. [*Back to* NICK] How do you like that for a declension, young man? Eh?

NICK: Sir, I'm sorry if we . . .

GEORGE [*with an edge in his voice*]: You didn't answer my question.

NICK: Sir?

GEORGE: Don't you condescend to me! [*Toying with him*] I asked you how you liked that for a declension: Good; better; best; bested. Hm? Well?

NICK [*with some distaste*]: I really don't know what to say.

GEORGE [*feigned incredulousness*]: You really don't know what to *say*?

NICK [*snapping it out*]: All right . . . what do you want me to say? Do you want me to say it's funny, so you can contradict me and say it's sad? Or do you want me to say it's sad so you can turn around and say no, it's funny. You can play that damn little game any way you want to, you know!

GEORGE [*feigned awe*]: Very good! Very good!

NICK [*even angrier than before*]: And when my wife comes back, I think we'll just . . .

GEORGE [*sincere*]: Now, now . . . calm down, my boy. Just . . . calm . . . down. [*Pause*] All right? [*Pause*] You want another drink? Here, give me your glass.

NICK: I still have one. I *do* think that when my wife comes downstairs . . .

GEORGE: Here . . . I'll freshen it. Give me your glass. [*Takes it.*]

NICK: What I mean is . . . you two . . . you and your wife . . . seem to be having *some* sort of a . . .

GEORGE: Martha and I are having . . . nothing. Martha and I are merely . . . exercising . . . that's all . . . we're merely walking what's left of our wits. Don't pay any attention to it.

NICK [*undecided*]: Still . . .

GEORGE [*an abrupt change of pace*]: Well, now . . . let's sit down and talk, hunh?

NICK [*cool again*]: It's just that I don't like to . . . become involved . . . [*An afterthought.*] uh . . . in other people's affairs.

GEORGE [*comforting a child*]: Well, you'll get over that . . . small college and all. Musical beds is the faculty sport around here.

NICK: Sir?

GEORGE: I said, musical beds is the faculty . . . Never mind. I wish you wouldn't go 'Sir' like that. . . not with the question-mark at the end of it. You know? Sir? I know it's meant to be a sign of respect for your [*Winces.*] elders . . . but . . . uh . . . the way you do it. . . . Uh . . . Sir? . . . Madam?

NICK [*with a small, noncommittal smile*]: No disrespect intended.

GEORGE: How old *are* you?

NICK: Twenty-eight.

GEORGE: I'm forty-something. [*Waits for reaction . . . gets none.*] Aren't you surprised? I mean . . . don't I look older? Doesn't this . . . *grey* quality suggest the fifties? Don't I sort of fade into backgrounds . . . get lost in the cigarette smoke? Hunh?

NICK [*looking around for an ashtray*]: I think you look . . . fine.

GEORGE: I've always been lean . . . I haven't put on five pounds since I was your age. I don't have a paunch, either.

. . . What I've got . . . I've got this little distension just below the belt. . . but it's hard. . . . It's not soft flesh. I use the handball courts. How much do *you* weigh?

NICK: I . . .

GEORGE: Hundred and fifty-five, sixty . . . something like that? Do you play handball?

NICK: Well, yes . . . no . . . I mean, not very well.

GEORGE: Well, then . . . we shall play some time. Martha is a hundred and eight . . . years *old*. She weighs somewhat more than that. How old is *your* wife?

NICK [*a little bewildered*]: She's twenty-six.

GEORGE: Martha is a remarkable woman. I would imagine she weighs around a hundred and ten.

NICK: Your . . . wife . . . weighs . . . ?

GEORGE: No, no, my boy. Yours! *Your* wife. My wife is Martha.

NICK: Yes . . . I know.

GEORGE: If you were married to Martha you would know what it means. [*Pause*] But then, if I were married to your wife I would know what that means, too . . . wouldn't I?

NICK [*after a pause*]: Yes.

GEORGE: Martha says you're in the Math Department, or something.

NICK [*as if for the hundredth time*]: No . . . I'm not.

GEORGE: Martha is seldom mistaken . . . maybe you *should* be in the Math Department, or something.

NICK: I'm a biologist. I'm in the Biology Department.

GEORGE [*after a pause*]: Oh. [*Then, as if remembering something*] OH!

NICK: Sir?

GEORGE: You're the one! You're the one's going to make all that trouble . . . making everyone the same, rearranging the chromozones, or whatever it is. Isn't that right?

NICK [*with that small smile*]: Not exactly: chromo*somes,*

GEORGE: I'm very mistrustful. Do you believe . . . [*Shifting in his chair*] . . . do you believe that people learn nothing from history? Not that there is nothing to learn, mind you, but that people learn nothing? I am in the History Department.

NICK: Well . . .

GEORGE: I am a Doctor. A.B. . . . M.A. . . . PH.D. . . . ABMAPHID! Abmaphid has been variously described as a wasting disease of the frontal lobes, and as a wonder drug. It is actually both. I'm really very mistrustful. Biology, hunh?

[NICK *does not answer . . . nods . . . looks.*]

I read somewhere that science fiction is really not fiction at all . . . that you people are rearranging my genes, so that everyone will be like everyone else. Now, I won't have that! It would be a . . . shame. I mean . . . look at me! Is it really such a good idea . . . if everyone was forty-something and looked fifty-five? You didn't answer my question about history.

NICK: This genetic business you're talking about . . .

GEORGE: Oh, that. [*Dismisses it with a wave of his hand.*] That's very upsetting . . . very . . . disappointing. But history is a great deal more . . . disappointing. I am in the History Department.

NICK: Yes . . . you told me.

GEORGE: I know I told you . . . I shall probably tell you several more times. Martha tells me often, that I am *in* the History Department . . . as opposed to *being* the History Department . . . in the sense of *running* the History Department. I do not run the History Department.

NICK: Well, I don't run the Biology Department.

GEORGE: You're twenty-one!

NICK: Twenty-eight.

GEORGE: Twenty-eight! Perhaps when you're forty-something and look fifty-five, you will run the History Department. . . .

NICK: . . . Biology. . . .

GEORGE: . . . the Biology Department. I *did* run the History Department, for four years, during the war, but that was because everybody was away. Then . . . everybody came back . . . because nobody got killed. That's New England for you. Isn't that amazing? Not one single man in this whole place got his head shot off. That's pretty irrational. [*Broods.*] Your wife *doesn't* have any hips . . . has she . . . does she?

NICK: What?

GEORGE: I don't mean to suggest that I'm hip-happy. . . . I'm not one of those thirty-six, twenty-two, seventy-eight men. No-siree . . . not me. Everything in proportion. I was implying that your wife is . . . slim-hipped.

NICK: Yes . . . she is.

GEORGE [*looking at the ceiling*]: What are they *doing* up there? I assume that's where they are.

NICK [*false heartiness*]: You know women.

GEORGE [*gives* NICK *a long stare, of feigned incredulity . . . then his attention moves*]: Not one son-of-a-bitch got killed. Of course, nobody bombed Washington. No . . . that's not fair. You have any kids?

NICK: Uh . . . no . . . not yet. [*Pause*] You?

GEORGE [*a kind of challenge*]: That's for me to know and you to find out.

NICK: Indeed?

GEORGE: No kids, hunh?

NICK: Not yet.

GEORGE: People do . . . uh . . . have kids. That's what I meant about history. You people are going to make them in test tubes, aren't you? You biologists. Babies. Then the rest of us . . . them as wants to . . . can screw to their heart's content. What will happen to the tax deduction? Has anyone figured that out yet?

[NICK, *who can think of nothing better to do, laughs mildly.*]

But you *are* going to have kids . . . anyway. In spite of
history.

NICK [*hedging*]: Yes . . . certainly. We . . . want to wait . . . a
little . . . until we're settled.

GEORGE: And this . . . [*With a handsweep taking in not only
the room, the house, but the whole countryside*] . . . this is
your heart's content – Illyria . . . Penguin Island . . .
Gomorrah. . . . You think you're going to be happy here in
New Carthage, eh?

NICK [*a little defensively*]: I hope we'll stay here.

GEORGE: And every definition has its boundaries, eh? Well, it
isn't a bad college, I guess. I mean . . . it'll do. It isn't
M.I.T. . . . it isn't U.C.L.A. . . . it isn't the Sorbonne . . . or
Moscow U. either, for that matter.

NICK: I don't mean . . . for ever.

GEORGE: Well, don't you let that get bandied about. The old
man wouldn't like it. Martha's father expects loyalty and
devotion out of his . . . staff. I was going to use another
word. Martha's father expects his . . . staff . . . to cling to
the walls of this place, like the ivy . . . to come here and
grow old . . . to fall in the line of service. One man, a
professor of Latin and Elocution, actually fell in the
cafeteria line, one lunch. He was buried, as many of us have
been, and as many more of us will be, under the shrubbery
around the chapel. It is said . . . and I have no reason to
doubt it . . . that we make excellent fertilizer. But the old
man is not going to be buried under the shrubbery . . . the
old man is not going to die. Martha's father has the staying
power of one of those Micronesian tortoises. There are
rumours . . . which you must not breathe in front of
Martha, for she foams at the mouth . . . that the old man,
her father, is over two hundred years old. There is probably
an irony involved in this, but I am not drunk enough to
figure out what it is. How many kids you going to have?

NICK: I . . . I don't know. . . . My wife is . . .

GEORGE: Slim-hipped. [*Rises.*] Have a drink.

NICK: Yes.

GEORGE: MARTHA! [*No answer.*] DAMN IT! [*To* NICK] You asked me if I knew women. . . . Well, one of the things I do *not* know about them is what they talk about while the men are talking. [*Vaguely*] I must find out some time.

MARTHA'S VOICE: WHADD'YA WANT?

GEORGE [*to* NICK]: Isn't that a wonderful sound? What I mean is . . . what do you think they really *talk* about . . . or don't you care?

NICK: Themselves, I would imagine.

MARTHA'S VOICE: GEORGE?

GEORGE [*to* NICK]: Do you find women . . . puzzling?

NICK: Well. . . yes and no.

GEORGE [*with a knowing nod*]: Unh-hunh. [*Moves towards the hall, almost bumps into* HONEY, *re-entering.*] Oh! Well, here's one of you, at least.

[HONEY *moves towards* NICK, GEORGE *goes to the hall.*]

HONEY [*to* GEORGE]: She'll be right down. [*To* NICK] You must see this house, dear . . . this is such a wonderful old house.

NICK: Yes, I . . .

GEORGE: MARTHA!

MARTHA'S VOICE: FOR CHRIST'S SAKE, HANG ON A MINUTE, WILL YOU?

HONEY [*to* GEORGE]: She'll be right down . . . she's changing.

GEORGE [*incredulous*]: She's *what?* She's changing?

HONEY: Yes.

GEORGE: Her clothes?

HONEY: Her dress.

GEORGE [*suspicious*]: Why?

HONEY [*with a nervous little laugh*]: Why, I imagine she wants to be . . . comfortable.

GEORGE [*with a threatening look towards the hall*]: Oh she does, does she?

HONEY: Well, heavens, I should think . . .

GEORGE: YOU DON'T KNOW!

NICK [*as* HONEY *starts*]: You feel all right?

HONEY [*reassuring, but with the echo of a whine. A long-practised tone*]: Oh, yes, dear . . . perfectly fine.

GEORGE [*fuming . . . to* himself]: So she wants to be comfortable, does she? Well, we'll see about that.

HONEY [*to* GEORGE, *brightly*]: I didn't know until just a minute ago that you had a *son*.

GEORGE [*wheeling, as if struck from behind*]: WHAT?

HONEY: A son! I hadn't known.

NICK: You to know and me to find out. Well, he must be quite a big . . .

HONEY: Twenty-one . . . twenty-one tomorrow . . . tomorrow's his birthday.

NICK [*a victorious smile*]: Well!

GEORGE [*to* HONEY]: She told you about him?

HONEY [*flustered*]: Well, *yes*. Well, I mean . . .

GEORGE [*nailing it down*]: She told you about him.

HONEY [*a nervous giggle*]: Yes.

GEORGE [*strangely*]: You say she's changing?

HONEY: Yes. . . .

GEORGE: And she mentioned . . . ?

HONEY [*cheerful, but a little puzzled*]: . . . your son's birthday . . . yes.

GEORGE [*more or less to himself*]: O.K., Martha . . . O.K.

NICK: You look pale, Honey. Do you want a . . . ?

HONEY: Yes, dear . . . a little more brandy, maybe. Just a drop.

GEORGE: O.K., Martha.

NICK: May I use the . . . uh . . . bar?

GEORGE: Hm? Oh, yes . . . yes . . . by all means. Drink away . . . you'll need it as the years go on. [*For* MARTHA, *as if she were in the room*] You goddamn destructive . . .

HONEY [*to cover*]: What time is it, dear?

NICK: Two-thirty.

HONEY: Oh, it's so late . . . we *should* be getting home.

GEORGE [*nastily, but he is so preoccupied he hardly notices his own tone*]: For what? You keeping the babysitter up, or something?

NICK [*almost a warning*]: I told you we didn't have children.

GEORGE: Hm? [*Realizing*] Oh, I'm sorry. I wasn't even listening . . . or thinking . . . [*With a flick of his hand*] . . . whichever one applies.

NICK [*softly, to* HONEY]: We'll go in a little while.

GEORGE [*driving*]: Oh no, now . . . you mustn't. Martha is changing . . . and Martha is not changing for *me*. Martha hasn't changed for *me* in years. If Martha is changing, it means we'll be here for . . . days. You are being accorded an honour, and you must not forget that Martha is the daughter of our beloved boss. She is his . . . right ball, you might say.

NICK: You might not understand this . . . but I wish you wouldn't talk that way in front of my wife.

HONEY: Oh, now . . .

GEORGE [*incredulous*]: Really? Well, you're quite right. . . . We'll leave that sort of talk to Martha.

MARTHA [*entering*]: What sort of talk?

[MARTHA *has changed her clothes, and she looks, now, more comfortable and . . . and this is most important . . . most voluptuous.*]

GEORGE: There you are, my pet.

NICK [*impressed; rising*]: Well, now . . .

GEORGE: Why, Martha . . . your Sunday chapel dress!

HONEY [*slightly disapproving*]: Oh, that's most attractive.

MARTHA [*showing off*]: You like it? Good! [*To* GEORGE] What the hell do you mean screaming up the stairs at me like that?

GEORGE: We got lonely, darling . . . we got lonely for the soft purr of your little voice.

MARTHA [*deciding not to rise to it*]: Oh. Well, then, you just trot over to the barie-poo . . .

GEORGE [*taking the tone from her*]: . . . and make your little mommy a gweat big dwink.

MARTHA [*giggles*]: That's right. [*To* NICK] Well, did you two have a nice little talk? You men solve the problems of the world, as usual?

NICK: Well, no, we . . .

GEORGE [*quickly*]: What we did, actually, if you really want to know, what we did actually is try to figure out what you two were talking about.

[HONEY *giggles*, MARTHA *laughs.*]

MARTHA [*to* HONEY]: Aren't they something? Aren't these . . . [*Cheerfully disdainful*] . . . *men* the absolute end? [*To* GEORGE] Why didn't you sneak upstairs and listen in?

GEORGE: Oh, I wouldn't have *listened*, Martha . . . I would have *peeked*.

[HONEY *giggles*, MARTHA *laughs.*]

NICK [*to* GEORGE, *with false heartiness*]: It's a conspiracy.

GEORGE: And now we'll never know. Shucks!

MARTHA [*to* NICK, *as* HONEY *beams*]: Hey, you must be quite a boy, getting your Masters when you were . . . what? . . . twelve? You hear that, George?

NICK: Twelve and a half, actually. No, nineteen really. [*To* HONEY] Honey, you needn't have mentioned that. It . . .

HONEY: Ohhhh . . . I'm *proud* of you. . . .

GEORGE [*seriously, if sadly*]: That's very . . . impressive.

MARTHA [*aggressively*]: You're damned right!

GEORGE [*between his teeth*]: I said I was impressed, Martha. I'm beside myself with jealousy. What do you want me to do, throw up? [*To* NICK] That really is very impressive. [*To* HONEY] You should be right proud.

HONEY [*coy*]: Oh, he's a pretty nice fella.

GEORGE [*to* NICK]: I wouldn't be surprised if you *did* take over the History Department one of these days.

NICK: The Biology Department.

GEORGE: The *Biology* Department . . . of course. I seem preoccupied with history. Oh! What a remark. [*He strikes a pose, his hand over his heart, his head raised, his voice stentorian.*] 'I am preoccupied with history.'

MARTHA [*as* HONEY *and* NICK *chuckle*]: Ha, ha, ha, HA!

GEORGE [*with some disgust*]: I think I'll make *myself* a drink.

MARTHA: George is not preoccupied with *history*. . . . George is preoccupied with the *History Department*. George is preoccupied with the History Department because . . .

GEORGE: . . . because he is *not* the History Department, but is only *in* the History Department. We know, Martha . . . we went all through it while you were upstairs . . . getting up. There's no need to go through it again.

MARTHA: That's right, baby . . . keep it clean. [*To the others*] George is bogged down in the History Department. He's an old bog in the History Department, that's what George is. A bog. . . . A fen. . . . A.G.D. swamp. Ha, ha, ha, HA! A SWAMP! Hey, swamp! Hey SWAMPY!

GEORGE [*with a great effort he controls himself . . . then, as if she had said nothing more than 'George, dear' . . .*]: Yes, Martha? Can I get you something?

MARTHA [*amused at his game*]: Well . . . uh . . . sure, you can light my cigarette, if you're of a mind to.

GEORGE [*considers, then moves off*]: No . . . there are limits. I mean, man can put up with only so much without he descends a rung or two on the old evolutionary ladder . . . [*Now a quick aside to* NICK] . . . which is up your line . . . [*Then back to* MARTHA] . . . sinks, Martha, and it's a funny ladder . . . you can't reverse yourself. . . start back up once you're descending.

[MARTHA *blows him an arrogant kiss.*]

Now . . . I'll hold your hand when it's dark and you're afraid of the bogey man, and I'll tote your gin bottles out after midnight, so no one'll see . . . but I will not light your cigarette. And that, as they say, is that.

[*Brief silence.*]

MARTHA [*under her breath*]: Jesus! [*Then, immediately, to* NICK] Hey, you played football, hunh?

HONEY [*as* NICK *seems sunk in thought*]: Dear . . .

NICK: Oh! Oh, yes . . . I was a . . . quarterback . . . but I was much more . . . adept . . . at boxing, really.

MARTHA [*with great enthusiasm*]: BOXING! You hear that, George?

GEORGE [*resignedly*]: Yes, Martha.

MARTHA [*to* NICK, *with peculiar intensity and enthusiasm*]: You musta been pretty good at it . . . I mean, you don't look like you got hit in the face at all.

HONEY [*proudly*]: He was intercollegiate state middleweight champion.

NICK [*embarrassed*]: Honey . . .

HONEY: Well, you were.

MARTHA: You look like you still got a pretty good body *now*, too . . . is that right? Have you?

GEORGE [*intensely*]: Martha . . . decency forbids . . .

MARTHA [*to* GEORGE . . . *still staring at* NICK, *though*]: SHUT UP! [*Now, back to* NICK] Well, have, you? Have you kept your body?

NICK [*unselfconscious . . . almost encouraging her*]: It's still pretty good. I work out.

MARTHA [*with a half-smile*]: Do you!

NICK: Yeah.

HONEY: Oh, yes . . . he has a very . . . firm body.

MARTHA [*still with that smile . . . a private communication with* NICK]: Have you! Oh, I think that's very nice.

NICK [*narcissistic, but not directly for* MARTHA]: Well, you never know . . . [*Shrugs*] . . . you know . . . once you have it . . .

MARTHA: . . . you never know when it's going to come in handy.

NICK: I was going to say . . . why give it up until you have to.

MARTHA: I couldn't agree with you more.
   [*They both smile, and there is a rapport of some unformed sort established.*]
I couldn't agree with you more.
GEORGE: Martha, your obscenity is more than . . .
MARTHA: George, here, doesn't cotton much to body talk . . . do you, sweetheart? [*No reply.*] George isn't too happy when we get to muscle. You know . . . flat bellies, pectorals. . . .
GEORGE [*to* HONEY]: Would you like to take a walk around the garden?
HONEY [*chiding*]: Oh, now. . . .
GEORGE [*incredulous*]: You're amused? [*Shrugs.*] All right.
MARTHA: Paunchy over there isn't too happy when the conversation moves to muscle. How much do you weigh?
NICK: A hundred and fifty-five, a hundred and . . .
MARTHA: Still at the old middleweight limit, eh? That's pretty good. [*Swings around.*] Hey, George, tell 'em about the boxing match *we* had.
GEORGE [*slamming his drink down, moving towards the hall*]: Christ!
MARTHA: George! Tell 'em about it!
GEORGE [*with a sick look on his face*]: You tell them, Martha. You're good at it. [*Exits.*]
HONEY: Is he . . . all right?
MARTHA [*laughs*]: Him? Oh, sure. George and I had this boxing match . . . Oh, Lord, twenty years ago . . . a couple of years after we were married.
NICK: A boxing match? The two of you?
HONEY: Really?
MARTHA: Yup . . . the two of us . . . really.
HONEY [*with a little shivery giggle of anticipation*]: I can't imagine it.
MARTHA: Well, like I say, it was twenty years ago, and it wasn't in a ring, or anything like that, you know what I mean. It

was wartime, and Daddy was on this physical fitness kick . . . Daddy's always admired physical fitness . . . says a man is only part brain . . . he has a body, too, and it's his responsibility to keep both of them up . . . you know?

NICK: Unh-hunh.

MARTHA: Says the brain can't work unless the body's working, too.

NICK: Well, that's not exactly so. . . .

MARTHA: Well, maybe that *isn't* what he says . . . something like it. *But* . . . it was wartime, and Daddy got the idea all the men should learn how to box . . . self-defence. I suppose the idea was if the Germans landed on the coast, or something, the whole faculty'd go out and punch 'em to death. . . . I don't know.

NICK: It was probably more the principle of the thing.

MARTHA: No kidding. Anyway, so Daddy had a couple of us over one Sunday and we went out in the back, and Daddy put on the gloves himself. Daddy's a strong man. . . . Well, *you* know.

NICK: Yes . . . yes.

MARTHA: And he asked George to box with him. Aaaaannnnd . . . George didn't *want* to . . . probably something about not wanting to bloody-up his meal ticket. . . .

NICK: Unh-hunh.

MARTHA: . . . Anyway, George said he didn't want to, and Daddy was saying, 'Come on, young man . . . what sort of son-in-law *are* you?' . . . and stuff like that.

NICK: Yeah.

MARTHA: So, while this was going on . . . I don't know why I *did* it . . . I got into a pair of gloves myself . . . you know, I didn't lace 'em up, or anything . . . and I snuck up behind George, just kidding, and I yelled 'Hey, George!' and at the same time I let go sort of a roundhouse right . . . just kidding, you know?

NICK: Unh-hunh.

MARTHA: . . . and George wheeled around real quick, and he
caught it right in the jaw . . . POW! [NICK *laughs*.] I hadn't
meant it . . . honestly. Anyway . . . POW! Right in the jaw
. . . and he was off balance . . . he must have been . . . and
he stumbled back a few steps, and then, CRASH, he landed
. . . flat . . . in a huckleberry bush!

> [NICK *laughs*, HONEY *goes tsk, tsk, tsk, tsk, and shakes
> her head*.]

It was awful, really. It was funny, but it was awful.

> [*She thinks, gives a muffled laugh in rueful con-
> templation of the incident*.]

I think it's coloured our whole life. Really I do! It's an
excuse, anyway.

> [GEORGE *enters now, his hands behind his back. No one
> sees him*.]

It's what he uses for being bogged down, anyway . . . why
he hasn't *gone* anywhere.

> [GEORGE *advances*, HONEY *sees him*.]

MARTHA: And it was an *accident* . . . a real, goddamn
accident!

> [GEORGE *takes from behind his back a short-barrelled
> shotgun, and calmly aims it at the back of* MARTHA's
> *head*. HONEY *screams . . . rises*, NICK *rises, and, simul-
> taneously*, MARTHA *turns her head to face* GEORGE.
> GEORGE *pulls the trigger*.]

GEORGE: POW!!!

> [*Pop! From the barrel of the gun blossoms a large red
> and yellow Chinese parasol*. HONEY *screams again, this
> time less, and mostly from relief and confusion*.]

You're dead! Pow! You're dead!

NICK [*laughing*]: Good Lord.

> [HONEY *is beside herself*, MARTHA *laughs too . . . almost
> breaks down, her great laugh booming*. GEORGE *joins in
> the general laughter and confusion. It dies, eventually*.]

HONEY: Oh! My goodness!

MARTHA [*joyously*]: Where'd you get that, you bastard?

NICK [*his hand out for the gun*]: Let me see that, will you?
    [GEORGE *hands him the gun.*]

HONEY: I've never been so frightened in my life! Never!

GEORGE [*a trifle abstracted*]: Oh, I've had it awhile. Did you
    like that?

MARTHA [*giggling*]: You bastard.

HONEY [*wanting attention*]: I've *never* been so frightened . . .
    never.

NICK: This is quite a gadget.

GEORGE [*leaning over* MARTHA]: You liked that, did you?

MARTHA: Yeah . . . that was pretty good. [*Softer*] C'mon . . .
    give me a kiss.

GEORGE [*indicating* NICK *and* HONEY]: Later, sweetie.
    [*But* MARTHA *will not be dissuaded. They kiss,* GEORGE
    standing, leaning over MARTHA'S *chair. She takes his
    hand, places it on her stage-side breast. He breaks away.*]
    Oh-ho! That's what you're after, is it? What are we going
    to have . . . blue games for the guests? Hunh? Hunh?

MARTHA [*angry-hurt*]: You . . . prick!

GEORGE [*a Pyrrhic victory*]: Everything in its place, Martha
    . . . everything in its own good time.

MARTHA [*an unspoken epithet*]: You . . .

GEORGE [*over to* NICK, *who still has the gun*]: Here, let me
    show you . . . it goes back in, like this.
    [*Closes the parasol, reinserts it in the gun.*]

NICK: That's damn clever.

GEORGE [*puts the gun down*]: Drinks now! Drinks for all!
    [*Takes* NICK'S *glass without question . . . goes to*
    MARTHA.]

MARTHA [*still angry-hurt*]: I'm not finished.

HONEY [*as* GEORGE *puts out his hand for her glass*]: Oh, I
    think I need *something*.
    [*He takes her glass, moves back to the portable bar.*]

NICK: Is that Japanese?

GEORGE: Probably.

HONEY [*to* MARTHA]: I was never so frightened in my life. Weren't you frightened? Just for a second?

MARTHA [*smothering her rage at* GEORGE]: I don't remember.

HONEY: Ohhhh, now . . . I bet you were.

GEORGE: Did you really think I was going to kill you, Martha?

MARTHA [*dripping contempt*]: You? . . . Kill me? . . . That's a laugh.

GEORGE: Well, now, I might. . . some day.

MARTHA: Fat chance.

NICK [*as* GEORGE *hands him his drink*]: Where's the john?

GEORGE: Through the hall there . . . and down to your left.

HONEY: Don't you come back with any guns, or anything, now.

NICK [*laughs*]: Oh, no.

MARTHA: You don't need any props, do you, baby?

NICK: Unh-unh.

MARTHA [*suggestive*]: I'll bet not. No fake Jap gun for you, eh?

NICK [*smiles at* MARTHA. *Then, to* GEORGE, *indicating a side table near the hall*]: May I leave my drink here?

GEORGE [*as* NICK *exits without waiting for a reply*]: Yeah . . . sure . . . why not? We've got half-filled glasses everywhere in the house, wherever Martha forgets she's left them . . . in the linen closet, on the edge of the bathtub . . . I even found one in the freezer, once.

MARTHA [*amused in spite of herself*]: You did not!

GEORGE: *Yes* I did.

MARTHA [*ibid.*]: You did *not*!

GEORGE [*giving* HONEY *her brandy*]: Yes I *did*. [*To* HONEY] Brandy doesn't give you a hangover?

HONEY: I never mix. And then, I don't drink very much, either.

GEORGE [*grimaces behind her back*]: Oh . . . that's good.

Your . . . your husband was telling me all about the . . . chromosomes.

MARTHA [*ugly*]: The what?

GEORGE: The chromosomes, Martha . . . the genes, or whatever they are [*To* HONEY] You've got quite a . . . terrifying husband.

HONEY [*as if she's being joshed*]: Ohhhhhhhhh. . . .

GEORGE: No, really. He's quite terrifying, with his chromosomes, and all.

MARTHA: He's in the Math Department.

GEORGE: No, Martha . . . he's a biologist.

MARTHA [*her voice rising*]: He's in the *Math* Department!

HONEY [*timidly*]: Uh . . . biology.

MARTHA [*unconvinced*]: Are you *sure*?

HONEY [*with a little giggle*]: Well, I ought to. [*Then as an afterthought*] Be.

MARTHA [*grumpy*]: I suppose *so*. I don't know who said he was in the Math Department.

GEORGE: You did, Martha.

MARTHA [*by way of irritable explanation*]: Well, I can't be expected to remember *everything*. I meet fifteen new teachers and their goddamn wives . . . present company outlawed, of course . . . [HONEY *nods, smiles sillily*.] . . . and I'm supposed to remember *everything*. [*Pause*] So? He's a biologist. Good for him. Biology's even better. It's less . . . abstruse.

GEORGE: Abstract.

MARTHA: ABSTRUSE! In the sense of recondite. [*Sticks her tongue out at* GEORGE.] Don't you tell me words. Biology's even better. It's . . . right at the *meat* of things.

[NICK *re-enters*.]

You're right at the meat of things, baby.

NICK [*taking his drink from the side table*]: Oh?

HONEY [*with that giggle*]: They thought you were in the Math Department.

NICK: Well, maybe I ought to be.

MARTHA: You stay right where you are . . . you stay right at the . . . *meat* of things.

GEORGE: You're obsessed with that phrase, Martha. . . . It's ugly.

MARTHA [*ignoring* GEORGE . . . *to* NICK]: You stay right there. [*Laughs.*] Hell, you can take over the History Department just as easy from there as anywhere else. God knows, *some*body's going to take over the History Department, *some* day, and it ain't going to be Georgie-boy, there . . . that's for sure. Are ya, swampy . . . are ya, hunh?

GEORGE: In my mind, Martha, you are buried in cement, right up to your neck. [MARTHA *giggles.*] No . . . right up to your nose . . . that's much quieter.

MARTHA [*to* NICK]: Georgie-boy, here, says you're terrifying. Why are you terrifying?

NICK [*with a small smile*]: I didn't know I was.

HONEY [*a little thickly*]: It's because of your chromosomes, dear.

NICK: Oh, the chromosome business. . . .

MARTHA [*to* NICK]: What's all this about chromosomes?

NICK: Well, chromosomes are . . .

MARTHA: I know what chromosomes are, sweetie, I love 'em.

NICK: Oh. . . . Well, then.

GEORGE: Martha eats them . . . for breakfast . . . she sprinkles them on her cereal. [*To* MARTHA, *now*] It's very simple, Martha, this young man is working on a system whereby chromosomes can be altered . . . well not all by himself – he probably has one or two co-conspirators – the genetic make-up of a sperm cell changed, reordered . . . *to* order, actually . . . for hair and eye colour, stature, potency . . . I imagine . . . hairiness, features, health. . . and *mind*. Most important . . . Mind. All imbalances will be corrected, sifted out . . . propensity for various diseases will be gone, longevity assured. We will have a race of men . . .

test-tube-bred . . . incubator-born . . . superb and sublime.

MARTHA [*impressed*]: Hunh!

HONEY: How exciting!

GEORGE: *But!* Everyone will tend to be rather the same. . . .
Alike. Everyone . . . and I'm sure I'm not wrong here . . .
will tend to look like this young man *here*.

MARTHA: *That's* not a bad idea.

NICK [*impatient*]: All right, now. . . .

GEORGE: It will, on the surface of it, be all rather pretty . . .
quite jolly. But of course there will be a dank side to it, too.
A certain amount of regulation will be necessary . . . uh . . .
for the experiment to succeed. A certain number of sperm
tubes will have to be cut.

MARTHA: Hunh! . . .

GEORGE: Millions upon millions of them . . . millions of tiny
little slicing operations that will leave just the smallest scar,
on the underside of the scrotum [MARTHA *laughs.*] but
which will assure the sterility of the imperfect . . . the ugly,
the stupid . . . the . . . unfit.

NICK [*grimly*]: Now look . . . !

GEORGE: . . . with this, we will have, in time, a race of
glorious men.

MARTHA: Hunh!

GEORGE: I suspect we will not have much music, much
painting, but we will have a civilization of men, smooth,
blond, and right at the middleweight limit.

MARTHA: Awww. . . .

GEORGE: . . . a race of scientists and mathematicians, each
dedicated to and working for the greater glory of the super-
civilization.

MARTHA: Goody.

GEORGE: There will be a certain . . . loss of liberty, I imagine,
as a result of this experiment . . . but diversity will no longer
be the goal. Cultures and races will eventually vanish . . .
the ants will take over the world.

NICK: Are you finished?

GEORGE [*ignoring him*]: And I, naturally, am rather opposed to all this. History, which is my field . . . history, of which I am one of the most famous bogs . . .

MARTHA: Ha, ha, HA!

GEORGE: . . . will lose its glorious variety and unpredictability. I, and with me the . . . the surprise, the multiplexity, the sea-changing rhythm of . . . history, will be eliminated. There will be order and constancy . . . and I am unalterably opposed to it. I will not give up Berlin!

MARTHA: You'll give up Berlin, sweetheart. You going to defend it with your paunch?

HONEY: I don't see what Berlin has to *do* with anything.

GEORGE: There is a saloon in West Berlin where the bar-stools are five feet high. And the earth . . . the floor . . . is . . . so . . . far . . . below you. I will not give up things like that. No . . . I won't. I will fight you, young man . . . one hand on my scrotum, to be sure . . . but with my free hand I will battle you to the death.

MARTHA [*mocking, laughing*]: Bravo!

NICK [*to* GEORGE]: That's right. And I am going to be the wave of the future.

MARTHA: You bet you are, baby.

HONEY [*quite drunk – to* NICK]: I don't see why you want to do all those things, dear. You never told me.

NICK [*angry*]: Oh for God's sake!

HONEY [*shocked*]: OH!

GEORGE: The most profound indication of a social malignancy . . . no sense of humour. None of the monoliths could take a joke. Read history. I know something about history.

NICK [*to* GEORGE, *trying to make light of it all*]: You . . . you don't know much about science, do you?

GEORGE: I know something about history. I know when I'm being threatened.

MARTHA [*salaciously – to* NICK]: So, everyone's going to look like you, eh?

NICK: Oh, sure. I'm going to be a personal screwing machine!

MARTHA: Isn't that nice.

HONEY [*her hands over her ears*]: Dear, you mustn't . . . you mustn't . . . you mustn't.

NICK [*impatiently*]: I'm sorry, Honey.

HONEY: Such language. It's . . .

NICK: I'm *sorry*. All right?

HONEY [*pouting*]: Well . . . all right. [*Suddenly she giggles insanely, subsides. To* GEORGE] . . . When is your son? [*Giggles again.*]

GEORGE: What?

NICK [*distastefully*]: Something about your son.

GEORGE : SON!

HONEY: When is . . . where is your son . . . coming home? [*Giggles.*]

GEORGE: Ohhhh. [*Too formal*] Martha? When is our son coming home?

MARTHA: Never mind.

GEORGE: No, no . . . I want to know . . . you brought it out into the open. When is he coming home, Martha?

MARTHA: I said never mind. I'm sorry I brought it up.

GEORGE: Him up . . . not it. You brought *him* up. Well, more or less. When's the little bugger going to appear, hunh? I mean isn't tomorrow meant to be his birthday, or something?

MARTHA: I don't want to talk about it!

GEORGE [*falsely innocent*]: But Martha . . .

MARTHA: I DON'T WANT TO TALK ABOUT IT!

GEORGE: I'll bet you don't. [*To* HONEY *and* NICK] Martha does not want to talk about it . . . him. Martha is sorry she brought it up . . . him.

HONEY [*idiotically*]: When's the little bugger coming home? [*Giggles.*]

GEORGE: Yes, Martha . . . since you had the bad taste to bring the matter up in the first place . . . when *is* the little bugger coming home?

NICK: Honey, do you think you . . . ?

MARTHA: George talks disparagingly about the little bugger because . . . well, because he has problems.

GEORGE: The little bugger has problems? What problems has the little bugger got?

MARTHA: Not the little bugger . . . stop calling him that! You! You've got problems.

GEORGE [*feigned disdain*]: I've never heard of anything more ridiculous in my life.

HONEY: Neither have I!

NICK: Honey . . .

MARTHA: George's biggest problem about the little . . . ha, ha, ha, HA! . . . about our son, about our great big son, is that deep down in the private-most pit of his gut, he's not completely sure it's his own kid.

GEORGE [*deeply serious*]: My God, you're a wicked woman.

MARTHA: And I've told you a million times, baby . . . I wouldn't conceive with anyone but you . . . you know that, baby.

GEORGE: A deeply wicked person.

HONEY [*deep in drunken grief*]: My, my, my, my. Oh, my.

NICK: I'm not sure that this is a subject for . . .

GEORGE: Martha's lying. I want you to know that, right now. Martha's lying. [MARTHA *laughs.*] There are very few things in this world that I *am* sure of . . . national boundaries, the level of the ocean, political allegiances, practical morality . . . none of these would I stake my stick on any more . . . but the one thing in this whole sinking world that I am sure of is my partnership, my chromo-somological partnership in the . . . creation of our . . . blond-eyed, blue-haired . . . son.

HONEY: Oh, I'm so glad!

MARTHA: That was a very pretty speech, George.

GEORGE: Thank you, Martha.

MARTHA: You rose to the occasion . . . good. Real good.

HONEY: Well . . . real well.

NICK: Honey . . .

GEORGE: Martha knows . . . she knows better.

MARTHA [*proudly*]: I know better. I been to college like everybody else.

GEORGE: Martha been to college. Martha been to a convent when she were a little twig of a thing, too.

MARTHA: And I was an atheist. [*Uncertainly*] I still am.

GEORGE: Not an atheist, Martha . . . a pagan. [*To* HONEY *and* NICK] Martha is the only true pagan on the eastern seaboard. [MARTHA *laughs*.]

HONEY: Oh, that's nice. Isn't that nice, dear?

NICK [*humouring her*]: Yes . . . wonderful.

GEORGE: And Martha paints blue circles around her things.

NICK: You do?

MARTHA [*defensively, for the joke's sake*]: Sometimes. [*Beckoning*] You wanna see?

GEORGE [*admonishing*]: Tut, tut, tut.

MARTHA: Tut, tut yourself . . . you old floozie!

HONEY: He's not a floozie . . . he can't be a floozie . . . you're a floozie. [*Giggles*.]

MARTHA [*shaking a finger at* HONEY]: Now you watch yourself!

HONEY [*cheerfully*]: All right. I'd like a nipper of brandy, please.

NICK: Honey, I think you've had enough, now . . .

GEORGE: Nonsense! Everybody's ready, I think. [*Takes glasses, etc.*]

HONEY [*echoing* GEORGE]: Nonsense.

NICK [*shrugging*]: O.K.

MARTHA [*to* GEORGE]: Our son does *not* have blue hair . . . or blue eyes, for that matter. He has green eyes . . . like me.

GEORGE: He has blue eyes, Martha.

MARTHA [*determined*]: Green.

GEORGE [*patronizing*]: Blue, Martha.

MARTHA [*ugly*]: GREEN! [*To* HONEY *and* NICK] He has the
loveliest green eyes . . . they aren't all flaked with brown
and grey, you know . . . hazel . . . they're real green . . .
deep, pure green eyes . . . like mine.

NICK [*peers*]: Your eyes are . . . brown, aren't they?

MARTHA: Green! [*A little too fast*] Well, in some lights they
look brown, but they're green. Not green like his . . . more
hazel. George has watery blue eyes . . . milky blue.

GEORGE: Make up your mind, Martha.

MARTHA: I was giving you the benefit of the doubt. [*Now
back to the others*] Daddy has green eyes, too.

GEORGE: He does not! Your father has tiny red eyes . . . like
a white mouse. In fact, he *is* a white mouse.

MARTHA: You wouldn't dare say a thing like that if he was
here! You're a coward!

GEORGE [*to* HONEY *and* NICK]: You know . . . that great
shock of white hair, and those little beady red eyes . . . a
great big white mouse.

MARTHA: George hates Daddy. . . not for anything Daddy's
done to him, but for his own . . .

GEORGE [*nodding . . . finishing it for her*]: . . . inadequacies.

MARTHA [*cheerfully*]: That's right. You hit it . . . right on the
snout. [*Seeing* GEORGE *exiting*] Where do you think *you're*
going?

GEORGE: We need some more booze, angel.

MARTHA: Oh. [*Pause*] So, go.

GEORGE [*exiting*]: Thank you.

MARTHA [*seeing that* GEORGE *has gone*]: He's a good
bartender . . . a good bar nurse. The S.O.B., he hates my
father. You know that?

NICK [*trying to make light of it*]: Oh, come on.

MARTHA [*offended*]: You think I'm kidding? You think I'm
joking? I never joke . . . I don't have a sense of humour.

[*Almost pouting*] I have a fine sense of the ridiculous, but no sense of humour. [*Affirmatively*] I have no sense of humour!

HONEY [*happily*]: I haven't, either.

NICK [*half-heartedly*]: Yes, you have, Honey . . . a quiet one.

HONEY [*proudly*]: Thank you.

MARTHA: You want to know *why* the S.O.B. hates my father? You want me to tell you? All right. . . . I will now tell you why the S.O.B. hates my father.

HONEY [*swinging to some sort of attention*]: Oh, good!

MARTHA [*sternly,* to HONEY]: *Some* people feed on the calamities of others.

HONEY [*offended*]: They do not!

NICK: Honey. . . .

MARTHA: All right! Shut up! Both of you! [*Pause.*] All right, now. Mommy died early, see, and I sort of grew up with Daddy. [*Pause – thinks*] . . . I went away to school, and stuff, but I more or less grew up with him. Jesus, I admired that guy! I worshipped him . . . I absolutely worshipped him. I still do. And he was pretty fond of me, too . . . you know? We had a real . . . rapport going . . . a real rapport.

NICK: Yeah, yeah.

MARTHA: And Daddy built this college . . . I mean, he built it up from what it was . . . it's his whole life. He *is* the college.

NICK: Unh-hunh.

MARTHA: The college is him. You know what the endowment was when he took over, and what it is *now*? You look it up some time.

NICK: I know . . . I read about it. . . .

MARTHA: Shut up and listen . . . [*As an afterthought*] . . . cutie. So after I got done with college and stuff, I came back here and sort of . . . sat around, for a while. I wasn't married, or anything. Wellllll, I'd *been* married . . . sort of . . . for a week, my sophomore year at Miss Muff's Academy for Young Ladies . . . college. A kind of junior

Lady Chatterley arrangement, as it turned out . . . the marriage, [NICK *laughs.*] He mowed the lawn at Miss Muff's, sitting up there, all naked, on a big power mower, mowing away. But Daddy and Miss Muff got together and put an end to that . . . real quick . . . annulled . . . which is a laugh . . . because theoretically you can't get an annulment if there's entrance. Ha! Anyway, so I was revirginized, finished at Miss Muff's . . . where they had one less gardener's boy, and a real shame, that was . . . and I came back here and sort of sat around for a while. I was hostess for Daddy and I took care of him . . . and it was . . . nice. It was very nice.

NICK: Yes . . . yes.

MARTHA: What do you mean, yes, yes? How would you know?

[NICK *shrugs helplessly.*]

Lover.

[NICK *smiles a little.*]

And I got the idea, about then, that I'd marry into the college . . . which didn't seem to be quite as stupid as it turned out. I mean, Daddy had a sense of history . . . of . . . continuation. . . . Why don't you come over here and sit by me?

NICK [*indicating* HONEY, *who is barely with it*]: I . . . don't think I . . . should. . . . I . . .

MARTHA: Suit yourself. A sense of continuation . . . history . . . and he'd always had it in the back of his mind to . . . *groom* someone to take over . . . some time, when he quit. A succession . . . you know what I mean?

NICK: Yes, I do.

MARTHA: Which is natural enough. When you've made something, you want to pass it on, to somebody. So, I was sort of on the lookout, for . . . prospects with the new men. An heir-apparent. [*Laughs.*] It wasn't *Daddy's* idea that I had to necessarily marry the guy. I mean, I wasn't the albatross . . . you didn't have to take me to get the prize, or anything like that. It was something *I* had in the back of *my* mind. And a lot of the new men were married . . . naturally.

NICK: Sure.

MARTHA [*with a strange smile*]: Like you, baby.

HONEY [*a mindless echo*]: Like you, baby.

MARTHA [*ironically*]: But then George came along . . . along came George.

GEORGE [*re-entering, with liquor*]: And along came George, bearing hooch. What are you doing now, Martha?

MARTHA [*unfazed*]: I'm telling a story. Sit down . . . you'll learn something.

GEORGE [*stays standing. Puts the liquor on the portable bar*]: All rightie.

HONEY: You've come back!

GEORGE: That's right.

HONEY: Dear! He's come back!

NICK: Yes, I see . . . I see.

MARTHA: Where was I?

HONEY: I'm *so* glad.

NICK: Shhhhh.

HONEY [*imitating him*]: Shhhhh.

MARTHA: Oh yeah. And along came George. That's right. WHO was young . . . intelligent . . . and . . . bushy-tailed, and . . . sort of cute . . . if you can imagine it . . .

GEORGE: . . . and younger than you. . . .

MARTHA: . . . and younger than me. . . .

GEORGE: . . . by six years. . . .

MARTHA: . . . by six years. . . . It doesn't bother me, George. . . . And along he came, bright-eyed, into the History Department. And you know what I did, dumb cluck that I am? You know what I did? I fell for him.

HONEY [*dreamy*]: Oh, that's nice.

GEORGE: Yes, she did. You should have seen it. She'd sit

outside of my room, on the lawn, at night, and she'd howl and claw at the turf . . . I couldn't work.

MARTHA [*laughs, really amused*]: I actually fell for him . . . it . . . that, there.

GEORGE: Martha's a Romantic at heart.

MARTHA: That I am. So, I actually fell for him. And the match seemed . . . practical, too. You know, Daddy was looking for someone to . . .

GEORGE: Just a minute, Martha. . . .

MARTHA: . . . take over, some time, when he was ready to . . .

GEORGE [*stony*]: Just a minute, Martha.

MARTHA: . . . retire, and so I thought . . .

GEORGE: STOP IT, MARTHA!

MARTHA [*irritated*]: Whadda you want?

GEORGE [*too patiently*]: I'd thought you were telling the story of our courtship, Martha . . . I didn't know you were going to start in on the other business.

MARTHA [*so-thereish*]: Well, I am!

GEORGE: I wouldn't, if I were you.

MARTHA: Oh . . . you wouldn't? Well, you're not!

GEORGE: Now, you've already sprung a leak about you-know-what. . . .

MARTHA [*a duck*]: What? What?

GEORGE: . . . about the apple of our eye . . . the sprout. . . the little bugger . . . [*Spits it out*] . . . our *son* . . . and if you start on this other business, I warn you, Martha, it's going to make me angry.

MARTHA [*laughing at him*]: Oh, it is, is it?

GEORGE: I warn you.

MARTHA [*incredulous*]: You *what*?

GEORGE [*very quietly*]: I warn you.

NICK: Do you really think we have to go through . . . ?

MARTHA: I stand warned! [*Pause . . . then, to* HONEY *and* NICK] So, anyway, I married the S.O.B., and I had it all planned out. . . . He was the groom . . . he was going to be groomed. He'd take over some day . . . first, he'd take over the History Department, and then, when Daddy retired, he'd take over the college . . . you know? That's the way it was supposed to be.

[*To* GEORGE, *who is at the portable bar with his back to her*]

You getting angry, baby? Hunh? [*Now back*] That's the way it was *supposed* to be. Very simple. And Daddy seemed to think it was a pretty good idea, too. For a while. Until he watched for a couple of years! [*To* GEORGE *again*] You getting angrier? [*Now back*] Until he watched for a couple of years and started thinking maybe it wasn't such a good idea after all . . . that maybe Georgie-boy didn't have the *stuff* . . . that he didn't have it in him!

GEORGE [*still with his back to them all*]: Stop it, Martha.

MARTHA [*viciously triumphant*]: The hell I will! You see, George didn't have much . . . push . . . he wasn't particularly aggressive. In fact he was sort of a . . . [*Spits the word at* GEORGE's *back*] . . . a FLOP! A great . . . big . . . fat . . . FLOP!

[CRASH! *Immediately after* FLOP! GEORGE *breaks a bottle against the portable bar and stands there, still with his back to them all, holding the remains of the bottle by the neck. There is a silence, with everyone frozen. Then . . .*]

GEORGE [*almost crying*]: I said stop, Martha.

MARTHA [*after considering what course to take*]: I hope that was an empty bottle, George. You don't want to waste good liquor . . . not on your salary.

[GEORGE *drops the broken bottle on the floor, not moving.*]

Not on an Associate Professor's salary. [*To* NICK *and* HONEY] I mean, he'd be . . . no good . . . at trustees' dinners, fund raising. He didn't have any . . . personality, you know

what I mean? Which was disappointing to Daddy, as you can
imagine. So, here I am, stuck with this flop. . . .

GEORGE [*turning around*]: . . . don't go on, Martha. . . .

MARTHA: . . . this BOG in the History Department. . . .

GEORGE: . . . don't, Martha, don't. . . .

MARTHA [*her voice rising to match his*]: . . . who's married to the President's daughter, who's expected to *be* somebody, not just some nobody, some bookworm, somebody, who's so damn . . . comtemplative, he can't make anything out of himself, somebody without the guts to make anybody proud of him . . . ALL RIGHT, GEORGE!

GEORGE [*under her, then covering, to drown her*]: I said, don't. All right . . . all right: [*Sings*]
Who's afaid of Virginia Woolf,
Virginia Woolf,
Virginia Woolf,
Who's afraid of Virginia Woolf, early in the morning.

GEORGE *and* HONEY [*who joins him drunkenly*]:
Who's afraid of Virginia Woolf,
Virginia Woolf,
Virginia Woolf . . . [*etc.*]

MARTHA: STOP IT!
[*A brief silence.*]

HONEY [*rising, moving towards the hall*]: I'm going to be sick
. . . I'm going to be sick . . . I'm going to vomit.
[*Exits*]

NICK [*going after her*]: Oh, for God's sake!
[*Exits*]

MARTHA [*going after them, looks back at* GEORGE *contemptuously*]: Jesus! [*Exits.* GEORGE *is alone on stage.*]

CURTAIN

ACT TWO

WALPURGISNACHT

[GEORGE, *by himself*: NICK *re-enters*.]

NICK [*after a silence*]: I . . . guess . . . she's all right. [*No answer.*] She . . . really shouldn't drink. [*No answer.*] She's . . . frail. [*No answer.*] Uh . . . slim-hipped, as you'd have it. [GEORGE *smiles vaguely.*] I'm really very sorry.

GEORGE [*quietly*]: Where's my little yum yum? Where's Martha?

NICK: She's making coffee . . . in the kitchen. She . . . gets sick quite easily.

GEORGE [*preoccupied*]: Martha? Oh no, Martha hasn't been sick a day in her life, unless you count the time she spends in the rest home. . . .

NICK [*he, too, quietly*]: No, no; *my* wife . . . *my* wife gets sick quite easily. Your wife is Martha.

GEORGE [*with some rue*]: Oh, yes . . . I know.

NICK [*a statement of fact*]: She doesn't really spend any time in a rest home.

GEORGE: Your wife?

NICK: No. Yours.

GEORGE: Oh! Mine. [*Pause*] No, no, she doesn't . . . *I* would; I mean if I were . . . her . . . she . . . *I* would. But I'm not . . . and so I don't. [*Pause*] I'd like to, though. It gets pretty bouncy around here sometimes.

NICK [*coolly*]: Yes . . . I'm sure.

GEORGE: Well, you saw an example of it.

NICK: I try not to . . .

GEORGE: Get involved. Um? Isn't that right?

NICK: Yes . . . that's right.

GEORGE: I'd imagine not.

NICK: I find it . . . embarrassing.

GEORGE [*sarcastic*]: Oh, you do, hunh?

NICK: Yes. Really. Quite.

GEORGE [*mimicking him*]: Yes. Really. Quite. [*Then aloud, but to himself*] IT'S DISGUSTING!

NICK: Now look! I didn't have anything . . .

GEORGE: DISGUSTING! [*Quietly, but with great intensity*] Do you think I like having that . . . whatever-it-is . . . ridiculing me, tearing me down, in front of . . . [*Waves his hand in a gesture of contemptuous dismissal*] YOU? Do you think I *care* for it?

NICK [*cold – unfriendly*]: Well, no . . . I don't imagine you care for it at all.

GEORGE: Oh, you don't imagine it, hunh?

NICK [*antagonistic*]: No . . . I don't. I don't imagine you do!

GEORGE [*withering*]: Your sympathy disarms me . . . your . . . your compassion makes me weep! Large, salty, unscientific tears!

NICK [*with great disdain*]: I just don't see why you feel you have to subject *other* people to it.

GEORGE: *I?*

NICK: If you and your . . . wife . . . want to go at each other, like a couple of . . .

GEORGE: *I!* Why *I* want to!

NICK: . . . animals, I don't see why you don't do it when there aren't any . . .

GEORGE [*laughing through his anger*]: Why, you smug, self-righteous little . . .

NICK [*a genuine threat*]: CAN . . . IT . . . MISTER!
    [*Silence.*]
    Just . . . watch it!

GEORGE: . . . scientist.

NICK: I've never hit an older man.

GEORGE [*considers it*]: Oh. [*Pause*] You just hit younger men
. . . and children . . . women . . . birds. [*Sees that* NICK *is
not amused.*] Well, you're quite right, of course. It isn't the
prettiest spectacle . . . seeing a couple of middle-age types
hacking away at each other, all red in the face and winded,
missing half the time.

NICK: Oh, you two don't miss . . . you two are pretty good.
Impressive.

GEORGE: And impressive things impress you, don't they?
You're . . . easily impressed . . . sort of a . . . pragmatic
idealism.

NICK [*a tight smile*]: No, it's that sometimes I can admire
things that I don't admire. Now, flagellation isn't my idea
of good times, but . . .

GEORGE: . . . but you can admire a good flagellator . . . a real
pro.

NICK: Unh-hunh . . . yeah.

GEORGE: Your wife throws up a lot, eh?

NICK: I didn't say that. . . . I said she gets sick quite easily.

GEORGE: Oh. I thought by sick you meant . . .

NICK: Well, it's true . . . She . . . she does throw up a lot. Once
she starts . . . there's practically no stopping her. . . . I mean,
she'll go right on . . . for hours. Not all the time, but . . .
regularly.

GEORGE: You can tell time by her, hunh?

NICK: Just about.

GEORGE: Drink?

NICK: Sure. [*With no emotion, except the faintest distaste, as*
GEORGE *takes his glass to the bar*] I married her because
she was pregnant.

GEORGE [*pause*]: Oh? [*Pause*] But you said you didn't have
any children . . . When I asked you, you said . . .

NICK: She wasn't . . . really. It was a hysterical pregnancy. She
blew up, and then she went down.

GEORGE: And while she was up, you married her.

NICK: And then she went down.

[*They both laugh, and are a little surprised that they do.*]

GEORGE: Uh . . . bourbon *is* right.

NICK: Uh . . . yes, bourbon.

GEORGE [*at the bar, still*]: When I was sixteen and going to prep school, during the Punic Wars, a bunch of us used to go into New York on the first day of vacations, before we fanned out to our homes, and in the evening this bunch of us used to go to this gin mill owned by the gangster-father of one of us – for this was during the Great Experiment, or Prohibition, as it is more frequently called, and it was a bad time for the liquor lobby, but a fine time for the crooks and the cops – and we would go to this gin mill, and we would drink with the grown-ups and listen to the jazz. And one time, in the bunch of us, there was this boy who was fifteen, and he had killed his mother with a shotgun some years before – accidentally, completely accidentally, without even an unconscious motivation, I have no doubt, no doubt at all – and this one evening this boy went with us, and we ordered our drinks, and when it came his turn he said, I'll have bergin . . . give me some bergin, please . . . bergin and water. Well, we all laughed . . . he was blond and he had the face of a cherub, and we all laughed, and his cheeks went red and the colour rose in his neck, and the assistant crook who had taken our order told people at the next table what the boy had said, and then they laughed, and then more people were told and the laughter grew, and more people and more laughter, and no one was laughing more than us, and none of us more than the boy who had shot his mother. And soon, everyone in the gin mill knew what the laughter was about, and everyone started ordering bergin, and laughing when they ordered it. And soon, of course, the laughter became less general, but it did not subside, entirely, for a very long time, for always at this table or that someone would order bergin and a new area of laughter would rise. We drank free that night, and we were bought champagne by the management, by the gangster-father of one of us. And, of course, we suffered the next day, each of us, alone, on his train, away from New York, each of us with a grown-up's hangover . . . but it was the grandest day of my . . . youth.

[*Hands* NICK *a* drink on the word.]

NICK [*very quietly*]: Thank you. What . . . what happened to the boy . . . the boy who had shot his mother?

GEORGE: I won't tell you.

NICK: All right.

GEORGE: The following summer, on a country road, with his learner's permit in his pocket and his father on the front seat to his right, he swerved the car, to avoid a porcupine, and drove straight into a large tree.

NICK [*faintly pleading*]: No.

GEORGE: He was not killed, of course. And in the hospital, when he was conscious and out of danger, and when they told him that his father *was* dead, he began to laugh, I have been told, and his laughter grew and he would not stop, and it was not until after they jammed a needle in his arm, not until after that, until his consciousness slipped away from him, that his laughter subsided . . . stopped. And when he was recovered from his injuries enough so that he could be moved without damage should he struggle, he was put in an asylum. That was thirty years ago.

NICK: Is he . . . still there?

GEORGE: Oh, yes. And I'm told that for these thirty years he has . . . not . . . uttered . . . one . . . sound.

[*A rather long silence: five seconds, please.*]

MARTHA! [*Pause*] MARTHA!

NICK: I told you . . . she's making coffee.

GEORGE: For your hysterical wife, who goes up and down.

NICK: Went. Up and down.

GEORGE: Went. No more?

NICK: No more. Nothing.

GEORGE [*after a sympathetic pause*]: The saddest thing about
men. . . . Well, no, one of the saddest things about men is
the way they age . . . some of them. Do you know what it
is with insane people? Do you? . . . the quiet ones?

NICK: No.

GEORGE: They don't change . . . they don't grow old.

NICK: They must.

GEORGE: Well, eventually, probably, yes. But they don't . . .
in the usual sense. They maintain a . . . a firm-skinned
serenity . . . the . . . the under-use of everything leaves them
. . . quite whole.

NICK: Are you recommending it?

GEORGE: No. Some things are sad, though. [*Imitates a pep-
talker*] But ya jest gotta buck up an' face 'em, 'at's all. Buck
up! [*Pause*] Martha doesn't have hysterical pregnancies.

NICK: My wife had *one*.

GEORGE: Yes. Martha doesn't have pregnancies at all.

NICK: Well, no . . . I don't imagine so . . . now. Do you have
any other kids? Do you have any daughters, or anything?

GEORGE [*as if it's a great joke*]: Do we have any *what*?

NICK: Do you have any . . . I mean, do you have only one . . .
kid . . . uh . . . your son?

GEORGE [*with a private knowledge*]: Oh no . . . just one . . .
one boy . . . our son.

NICK: Well . . . [*Shrugs*] . . . that's nice.

GEORGE: Oh ho, ho. Yes, well, he's a . . . comfort, a bean bag.

NICK: A what?

GEORGE: A bean bag. Bean bag. You wouldn't understand
[*Over-distinct*] Bean . . . bag.

NICK: I *heard* you . . . I didn't say I was deaf. . . I said I didn't
understand.

GEORGE: You didn't say that at all.

NICK: I meant I was *implying* I didn't understand. [*Under his
breath*] For Christ's sake!

GEORGE: You're getting testy.

NICK [*testy*]: I'm sorry.

GEORGE: All I said was, our son . . . the apple of our three eyes, Martha being a Cyclops . . . our son is a bean bag, and you get testy.

NICK: I'm sorry! It's late, I'm tired, I've been drinking since nine o'clock, my wife is vomiting, there's been a lot of screaming going on around here. . . .

GEORGE: And so you're testy. Naturally. Don't . . . worry about it. Anybody who comes here ends up getting . . . testy. It's expected . . . don't be upset.

NICK [*testy*]: I'm not upset!

GEORGE: You're testy.

NICK: Yes.

GEORGE: I'd like to set you straight about something . . . while the little ladies are out of the room . . . I'd like to set you straight about what Martha said.

NICK: I don't . . . make judgements, so there's no need, really, unless you . . .

GEORGE: Well, I want to. I know you don't like to become involved . . . I know you like to . . . preserve your scientific detachment in the face of – for lack of a better word – life . . . and all . . . but still, I want to tell you.

NICK [*a tight, formal smile*]: I'm a . . . guest. You go right ahead.

GEORGE [*mocking appreciation*]: Oh . . . well, thanks. Now! That makes me feel all warm and runny inside.

NICK: Well, if you're going to . . .

MARTHA'S VOICE: HEY!

NICK: . . . if you're going to start that kind of stuff again. . .

GEORGE: Hark! Forest sounds.

NICK: Hm?

GEORGE: Animal noises.

MARTHA [*sticking her head in*]: Hey!

NICK: Oh!

GEORGE: Well, here's nursie.

MARTHA [to NICK]: We're sitting up . . . we're having coffee, and we'll be back in.

NICK [not rising]: Oh . . . is there anything I should do?

MARTHA: Nayh. You just stay here and listen to George's side of things. Bore yourself to death.

GEORGE: Monstre!

MARTHA: Cochon!

GEORGE: Bête!

MARTHA: Canaille!

GEORGE: Putain!

MARTHA [with a gesture of contemptuous dismissal]: Yaaaahhhh! You two types amuse yourselves . . . we'll be in. [As she goes] You clean up the mess you made, George?

GEORGE [MARTHA goes. GEORGE speaks to the empty hallway]: No, Martha, I did not clean up the mess I made. I've been trying for years to clean up the mess I made.

NICK: Have you?

GEORGE: Hm?

NICK: Have you been trying for years?

GEORGE [after a long pause . . . looking at him]: Accommodation, malleability, adjustment. . . those do seem to be in the order of things, don't they?

NICK: Don't try to put me in the same class with you!

GEORGE [pause]: Oh. [Pause] No, of course not. Things are simpler with you . . . you marry a woman because she's all blown up . . . while I, in my clumsy, old-fashioned way . . .

NICK: There was more to it than that!

GEORGE: Sure! I'll bet she has money, too!

NICK [looks hurt. Then, determined, after a pause]: Yes.

GEORGE: Yes? [Joyfully] YES! You mean I was right? I hit it?

NICK: Well, you see . . .

GEORGE: My God, what archery! First try, too. How about that!

NICK: You see . . .

GEORGE: There were other things.

NICK: Yes.

GEORGE: To compensate.

NICK: Yes.

GEORGE: There always are. [*Sees that* NICK *is reacting badly.*] No, I'm sure there are. I didn't mean to be . . . flip. There are *always* compensating factors . . . as in the case of Martha and myself. . . . Now, on the surface of it. . .

NICK: We sort of grew up together, you know . . .

GEORGE: . . .it looks to be a kind of knock-about, drag-out affair, on the *surface* of it. . .

NICK: We knew each other from, oh God, I don't know, when we were *six,* or something . . .

GEORGE: . . . but somewhere back there, at the beginning of it, right when I first came to New Carthage, back then . . .

NICK [*with some irritation*]: I'm *sorry.*

GEORGE: Hm? Oh. No, no . . . *I'm* sorry.

NICK: No . . . it's . . . it's all right.

GEORGE: No . . . you go ahead.

NICK: No . . . please.

GEORGE: I insist. . . . You're a guest. You go first.

NICK: Well, it seems a little silly . . . now.

GEORGE: Nonsense! [*Pause*] But if you were six, she must have been four, or something.

NICK: Maybe I was eight. . . she was six. We . . . we used to play . . . doctor.

GEORGE: That's a good healthy heterosexual beginning.

NICK [*laughing*]: Yup.

GEORGE: The scientist even then, eh?

NICK [*laughs*]: Yeah. And it was . . . always taken for granted . . . you know . . . by our families, and by us, too, I guess. And . . . so, we did.

GEORGE [*pause*]: Did what?

NICK: We got married.

GEORGE: When you were eight?

NICK: No. No, of course not. Much later.

GEORGE: I wondered.

NICK: I wouldn't say there was any . . . particular *passion* between us, even at the beginning . . . of our marriage, I mean.

GEORGE: Well, certainly no surprise, no earth-shaking discoveries, after Doctor, and all.

NICK [*uncertainly*]: No. . . .

GEORGE: Everything's all pretty much the same, anyway . . . in *spite* of what they say about Chinese women.

NICK: What is that?

GEORGE: Let me freshen you up. [*Takes* NICK's *glass.*]

NICK: Oh, thanks. After a while you don't get any drunker, do you?

GEORGE: Well, you *do* . . . but it's different . . . everything slows down. . . . you get sodden. . . . unless you can up-chuck . . . like your wife . . . then you can sort of start all over again.

NICK: Everybody drinks a lot here in the East. [*Thinks about it.*] Everybody drinks a lot in the middle-west, too.

GEORGE: We drink a great deal in this country, and I suspect we'll be drinking a great deal more, too . . . if we survive. We should be Arabs or Italians . . . the Arabs don't drink, and the Italians don't get drunk much, except on religious holidays. We should live on Crete, or something.

NICK [*sarcastically . . . as if killing a joke*]: And that, of course, would make us cretins.

GEORGE [*mild surprise*]: So it would. [*Hands* NICK *his drink.*] Tell me about your wife's money.

NICK [*suddenly suspicious*]: Why?

GEORGE: Well . . . don't, then.

NICK: What do you want to know about my wife's money for? [*Ugly.*] Hunh?

GEORGE: Well, I thought it would be nice.

NICK: No you didn't.

GEORGE [*still deceptively bland*]: All right. . . . I want to know about your wife's money because . . . well, because I'm fascinated by the methodology . . . by the pragmatic accommodation by which you wave-of-the-future boys are going to take over.

NICK: You're starting in again.

GEORGE: Am I? No I'm not. Look . . . Martha has money too. I mean, her father's been robbing this place blind for years, and . . .

NICK: No, he hasn't. He has not.

GEORGE: He hasn't?

NICK: No.

GEORGE [*shrugs*]: Very well. . . . Martha's father has *not* been robbing this place blind for years, and Martha does not have any money. O.K.?

NICK: We were talking about *my* wife's money . . . not yours.

GEORGE: O.K. . . . talk.

NICK: No. [*Pause*] My father-in-law . . . was a man of the Lord, and he was very rich.

GEORGE: What faith?

NICK: He . . . my father-in-law . . . was called by God when he was six, or something, and he started preaching, and he baptized people, and he saved them, and he travelled around a lot, and he became pretty famous . . . not like some of them, but he became pretty famous . . . and when he died he had a lot of money.

GEORGE: God's money.

NICK: No . . . his own.

GEORGE: What happened to God's money?

NICK: He spent God's money . . . and he saved his own. He built hospitals, and he sent off Mercy ships, and he brought the outhouses indoors, and he brought the people out-doors, into the sun, and he built three churches, or whatever they were, and two of them burned down . . . and he ended up pretty rich.

GEORGE [*after considering it*]: Well, I think that's very nice.

NICK: Yes. [*Pause. Giggles a little.*] And so, my wife's got some money.

GEORGE: But not God's money.

NICK: No. Her own.

GEORGE: Well, I think that's very nice.

[NICK *giggles a little.*]

Martha's got money because Martha's father's second wife . . . not Martha's mother, but after Martha's mother died . . . was a very old lady with warts who was very rich.

NICK: She was a witch.

GEORGE: She was a *good* witch, and she married the white mouse. . .

[NICK *begins to giggle.*]

. . . with the tiny red eyes . . . and he must have nibbled her warts, or something like that, because she went up in a puff of smoke almost immediately, POUF!

NICK: POUF!

GEORGE: POUF! And all that was left, aside from some wart medicine, was a big fat will. . . . A peach pie, with some for the township of New Carthage, some for the college, some for Martha's daddy, and just this much for Martha.

NICK [*quite beside himself*]: Maybe . . . maybe my father-in-law and the witch with the warts should have gotten together, because he was a mouse, too.

GEORGE [*urging* NICK *on*]: He was?

NICK [*breaking down*]: Sure . . . he was a church mouse! [*They both laugh a great deal, but it is sad laughter . . . eventually they subside, fall silent.*] Your wife never mentioned a stepmother.

GEORGE [*considers it*]: Well . . . maybe it isn't true.

NICK [*narrowing his eyes*]: And maybe it is.

GEORGE: Might be . . . might not. Well, I think your story's a lot nicer . . . about your pumped-up little wife, and your father-in-law who was a priest. . . .

NICK: He was not a priest . . . he was a man of God.

GEORGE: Yes.

NICK: And my wife wasn't pumped up . . . she blew up.

GEORGE: Yes, yes.

NICK [giggling]: Get things straight.

GEORGE: I'm sorry . . . I will. I'm sorry.

NICK: O.K.

GEORGE: You realize, of course, that I've been drawing you out on this stuff, not because I'm interested in your terrible lifehood, but only because you represent a direct and pertinent threat to my lifehood, and I want to get the goods on you.

NICK [still amused]: Sure . . . sure.

GEORGE: I mean . . . I've warned you . . . you stand warned.

NICK: I stand warned. [Laughs.] It's you sneaky types worry me the most, you know. You ineffectual sons of bitches . . . you're the worst.

GEORGE: Yes . . . we are. Sneaky. An elbow in your steely-blue eye . . . a knee in your solid gold groin . . . we're the worst.

NICK: Yup.

GEORGE: Well, I'm glad you don't believe me. . . . I know you've got history on your side, and all. . . .

NICK: Unh-unh. You've got history on your side. . . . I've got biology on mine. History, biology.

GEORGE: I know the difference.

NICK: You don't act it.

GEORGE: No? I thought we'd decided that you'd take over the History Department first, before you took over the whole works. You know . . . a step at a time.

NICK [stretching . . . luxuriating . . . playing the game]: Nyaah . . . what I thought I'd do is . . . I'd sort of insinuate myself generally, play around for a while, find all the weak spots, shore 'em up, but with my own name plate on 'em . . . become sort of a fact, and then turn into a . . . a what . . . ?

GEORGE: An inevitability.

NICK: Exactly. . . . An inevitability. You know. . . . Take over a few courses from the older men, start some special groups for myself. . . plough a few pertinent wives. . . .

GEORGE: Now that's it! You can take over all the courses you want to, and get as much of the young elite together in the gymnasium as you like, but until you start ploughing pertinent wives, you really aren't working. The way to a man's heart is through his wife's belly, and don't you forget it.

NICK [*playing along*]: Yeah. . . . I know.

GEORGE: And the women around here are no better than puntas – you know, South American ladies of the night. You know what they do in South America . . . in Rio? The puntas? Do you know? They hiss . . . like geese. . . . They stand around in the street and they hiss at you . . . like a bunch of geese.

NICK: Gangle.

GEORGE: Hm?

NICK: Gangle . . . gangle of geese . . . not bunch. . . gangle.

GEORGE: Well, if you're going to get all cute about it, all ornithological, it's gaggle . . . not gangle, *gaggle*.

NICK: Gaggle? Not Gangle?

GEORGE: Yes, gaggle.

NICK [*crestfallen*]: Oh.

GEORGE: Oh. Yes. . . . Well they stand around on the street and they hiss at you, like a bunch of geese. All the faculty wives, downtown in New Carthage, in front of the A&P, hissing away like a bunch of geese. That's the way to power – plough 'em all!

NICK [*still playing along*]: I'll bet you're right.

GEORGE: Well, I am.

NICK: And I'll bet your wife's the biggest goose in the gangle, isn't she . . . ? Her father president, and all.

GEORGE: You bet your historical inevitability she is!

NICK: Yessirree. [*Rubs his hands together.*] Well now, I'd just better get her off in a corner and mount her like a goddamn dog, eh?

GEORGE: Why, you'd certainly better.

NICK [*looks at* GEORGE *a minute, his expression a little sick*]: You know, I almost think you're serious.

GEORGE [*toasting him*]: No, baby. . . *you* almost think you're serious, and it scares the hell out of you.

NICK [*exploding in disbelief*]: ME!

GEORGE [*quietly*]: Yes . . . you.

NICK: You're kidding!

GEORGE [*like a father*]: I wish I were. . . . I'll give you some good advice if you want me to. . . .

NICK: Good advice! From you? Oh boy! [*Starts to laugh.*]

GEORGE: You haven't learned yet. . . . Take it wherever you can get it. . . . Listen to me, now.

NICK: Come off it!

GEORGE: I'm giving you good advice, now.

NICK: Good God . . . !

GEORGE: There's quicksand here, and you'll be dragged down, just as . . .

NICK: Oh boy . . . !

GEORGE: . . . before you know it. . . sucked down. . . .
     [NICK *laughs derisively.*]
You disgust me on principle, and you're a smug son of a bitch personally, but I'm trying to give you a survival kit. DO YOU HEAR ME?

NICK [*still laughing*]: I hear you. You come in loud.

GEORGE: ALL RIGHT!

NICK: Hey, Honey.

GEORGE [*silence. Then quietly*]: All right . . . O.K. You want to play it by ear, right? Everything's going to work out anyway, because the time-table's history, right?

NICK: Right. . . right. You just tend to your knitting, grandma. . . . I'll be O.K.

GEORGE [*after a silence*]: I've tried to . . . tried to reach you . . . to . . .

NICK [*contemptuously*]: . . . make contact?

GEORGE: Yes.

NICK [*still*]: . . . communicate?

GEORGE: Yes. Exactly.

NICK: Aw . . . that *is* touching . . . that is . . . downright moving . . . that's what it is. [*With sudden vehemence*] UP YOURS!

GEORGE [*brief pause*]: Hm?

NICK [*threatening*]: You heard me!

GEORGE [*at* NICK, *not to him*]: You take the trouble to construct a civilization . . . to . . . to build a society, based on the principles of . . . of principle . . . you endeavour to make communicable sense out of natural order, morality out of the unnatural disorder of man's mind . . . you make government and art, and realize that they are, must be, both the same . . . you bring things to the saddest of all points . . . to the point where there *is* something to lose . . . then all at once, through all the music, through all the sensible sounds of men building, attempting, comes the *Dies Irae*. And what is it? What does the trumpet sound? Up yours. I suppose there's justice to it, after all the years. . . . Up yours.

NICK [*brief pause . . . then applauding*]: Ha, ha! Bravo! Ha, ha! [*Laughs on.*]

     [*And* MARTHA *re-enters, leading* HONEY, *who is wan but smiling bravely.*]

HONEY [*grandly*]: Thank you . . . thank you.

MARTHA: Here we are, a little shaky, but on our feet.

GEORGE: Goodie.

NICK: What? Oh . . . OH! Hi, Honey . . . you better?

HONEY: A little bit, dear. . . . I'd better sit down, though.

NICK: Sure . . . c'mon . . . you sit by me.

HONEY: Thank you, dear.

GEORGE [*beneath his breath*]: Touching . . . touching.

MARTHA [*to* GEORGE]: Well? Aren't you going to apologize?

GEORGE [*squinting*]: For what, Martha?

MARTHA: For making the little lady throw up, what else?

GEORGE: I did not make her throw up.

MARTHA: You most certainly did!

GEORGE: I did not!

HONEY [*papal gesture*]: No, now . . . no.

MARTHA [*to* GEORGE]: Well, who do you think did . . . Sexy over there? You think he made his *own* little wife sick?

GEORGE [*helpfully*]: Well, you make *me* sick.

MARTHA: THAT'S DIFFERENT!

HONEY: No, now. I . . . I throw up . . . I mean, I get sick . . . occasionally, all by myself . . . without any reason.

GEORGE: Is that a fact?

NICK: You're . . . you're delicate, Honey.

HONEY [*proudly*]: I've always done it.

GEORGE: Like Big Ben.

NICK [*a warning*]: Watch it!

HONEY: And the doctors say there's nothing wrong with me . . . organically. You know?

NICK: Of course there isn't.

HONEY: Why, just before we got married, I developed . . . appendicitis . . . or everybody *thought* it was appendicitis . . . but it turned out to be . . . it was a . . . [*Laughs briefly.*] . . . false alarm.

  [GEORGE *and* NICK *exchange glances.*]

MARTHA [*to* GEORGE]: Get me a drink.

  [GEORGE *moves to the bar.*]

  George makes everybody sick. . . . When our son was just a little boy, he used to . . .

GEORGE: Don't, Martha. . . .

MARTHA: . . . he used to throw up all the time, because of George. . . .

GEORGE: I said, don't!

MARTHA: It got so bad that whenever George came into the room he'd start right in retching, and . . .

GEORGE: . . . the real reason [*Spits out the words*] our son . . . used to throw up all the time, wife and lover, was nothing more complicated than that he couldn't stand you fiddling at him all the time, breaking into his bedroom with your kimono flying, fiddling at him all the time, with your liquor breath on him, and your hands all over his . . .

MARTHA: YEAH? And I suppose that's why he ran away from home twice in one month, too. [*Now to the guests*] Twice in one month! Six times in one year!

GEORGE [*also to the guests*]: Our son ran away from home all the time because Martha here used to corner him.

MARTHA [*braying*]: I NEVER CORNERED THE SON OF A BITCH IN MY LIFE!

GEORGE [*handing* MARTHA *her drink*]: He used to run up to me when I'd get home, and he'd say, 'Mama's always coming at me.' That's what he'd say.

MARTHA: Liar!

GEORGE [*shrugging*]: Well, that's the way it was . . . you were always coming at him. I thought it was very embarrassing.

NICK: If you thought it was so embarrassing, what are you talking about it for?

HONEY [*admonishing*]: Dear . . . !

MARTHA: Yeah! [*To* NICK] Thanks, sweetheart.

GEORGE [*to them all*]: I didn't want to talk about him at all . . . I would have been perfectly happy not to discuss the whole subject. . . . I never want to talk about it.

MARTHA: Yes you do.

GEORGE: When we're alone, maybe.

MARTHA: We're alone!

GEORGE: Uh . . . no, love . . . we've got guests.

MARTHA [*with a covetous look at* NICK]: We sure have.

HONEY: Could I have a little brandy? I think I'd like a little brandy.

NICK: Do you think you should?

HONEY: Oh yes . . . yes, dear.

GEORGE [*moving to the bar again*]: Sure! Fill 'er up!

NICK: Honey, I don't think you . . .

HONEY [*petulance creeping in*]: It will steady me, *dear*. I feel a little unsteady.

GEORGE: Hell, you can't walk steady on half a bottle . . . got to do it right.

HONEY: Yes. [*To* MARTHA] I love brandy . . . I really do.

MARTHA [*somewhat abstracted*]: Good for you.

NICK [*giving up*]: Well, if you think it's a good idea . . .

HONEY [*really testy*]: I know what's best for me, dear.

NICK [*not even pleasant*]: Yes . . . I'm sure you do.

HONEY [GEORGE *hands her a brandy*]: Oh, goodie! Thank you. [*To* NICK] Of course I do, dear.

GEORGE [*pensively*]: I used to drink brandy.

MARTHA [*privately*]: You used to drink bergin, too.

GEORGE [*sharp*]: Shut up, Martha!

MARTHA [*her hand over her mouth in a little girl gesture*]: Oooooops.

NICK [*something having clicked, vaguely*]: Hm?

GEORGE [*burying it*]: Nothing . . . nothing.

MARTHA [*she, too*]: You two men have it out while we were gone? George tell you his side of things? He bring you to tears, hunh?

NICK: Well . . . no. . . .

GEORGE: No, what we did, actually, was . . . we sort of danced around.

MARTHA: Oh, yeah? Cute!

HONEY: Oh, I love dancing.

NICK: He didn't mean that, Honey.

HONEY: Well, I didn't think he did! Two grown men dancing . . . heavens!

MARTHA: You mean he didn't start in on how he would have amounted to something if it hadn't been for Daddy? How his high moral sense wouldn't even let him *try* to better himself? No?

NICK [*qualified*]: No. . . .

MARTHA: And he didn't run on about how he tried to publish a goddamn book, and Daddy wouldn't let him.

NICK: A book? No.

GEORGE: Please, Martha. . . .

NICK [*egging her on*]: A book? What book?

GEORGE [*pleading*]: Please. Just a book.

MARTHA [*mock incredulity*]: Just a book!

GEORGE: *Please,* Martha!

MARTHA [*almost disappointed*]: Well, I guess you didn't get the whole sad story. What's the matter with you, George? You given up?

GEORGE [*calm . . . serious*]: No . . . no. It's just I've got to figure out some new way to fight you, Martha. Guerilla tactics, maybe . . . internal subversion . . . I don't know. Something.

MARTHA: Well, you figure it out, and you let me know when you do.

GEORGE [*cheery*]: All right, love.

HONEY: Why don't we dance? I'd love some dancing.

NICK: Honey. . . .

HONEY: I would! I'd love some dancing.

NICK: Honey . . .

HONEY: I *want* some! I want some dancing!

GEORGE: All right. . .! For heaven's sake . . . we'll have some dancing.

HONEY [*all sweetness again. To* MARTHA]: Oh, I'm so glad . . . I just love dancing. Don't you?

MARTHA [*with a glance at* NICK]: Yeah . . . yeah, that's not a bad idea.

NICK [*genuinely nervous*]: Gee.

GEORGE: Gee.

HONEY: I dance like the wind.

MARTHA [*without comment*]: Yeah?

GEORGE [*picking a record*]: Martha had her daguerrotype in the paper once . . . oh, 'bout twenty-five years ago. . . . Seems she took second prize in one o' them seven-day dancin' contest things . . . biceps all bulging, holding up her partner.

MARTHA: Will you put a record on and shut up?

GEORGE: Certainly, love. [*To all*] How are we going to work this? Mixed doubles?

MARTHA: Well, you certainly don't think I'm going to dance with *you*, do you?

GEORGE [*considers it*]: Noooooo . . . not with him around . . . that's for sure. And not with twinkle-toes here, either.

HONEY: I'll dance with anyone . . . I'll dance by myself.

NICK: Honey. . . .

HONEY: I dance like the wind.

GEORGE: All right, kiddies . . . choose up and hit the sack.
[*Music starts. . . . Second movement, Beethoven's 7th Symphony.*]

HONEY [*up, dancing by herself*]: De, de de *da* da, da-da de, da *da-da* de da . . . wonderful. . . !

NICK: Honey. . . .

MARTHA: All right, George . . . cut that out!

HONEY: Dum, de de da da, da-da de, dum de *da* da da Wheeeee . . . !

MARTHA: Cut it out, George!

GEORGE [*pretending not to hear*]: What, Martha? What?

NICK: Honey. . . .

MARTHA [*as* GEORGE *turns up the volume*]: CUT IT OUT, GEORGE!

GEORGE: WHAT?

MARTHA [*gets up, moves quickly, threateningly, to* GEORGE]: All right, you son of a bitch. . . .

GEORGE [*record off, at once. Quietly*]: What did you say, love?

MARTHA: You son of a . . .

HONEY [*in an arrested posture*]: You stopped! Why did you stop?

NICK: Honey. . . .

HONEY [*to* NICK, *snapping*]: Stop that!

GEORGE: I thought it was fitting, Martha.

MARTHA: Oh you did, hunh?

HONEY: You're always *at* me when I'm having a good time.

NICK [*trying to remain civil*]: I'm sorry, Honey.

HONEY: Just . . . leave me alone!

GEORGE: Well, why don't *you* choose, Martha? [*Moves away from the phonograph . . . leaves it to* MARTHA.] Martha's going to run things . . . the little lady's going to lead the band.

HONEY: I like to dance and you don't want me to.

NICK: *I* like you to dance.

HONEY: Just. . . leave me alone. [*She sits . . . takes a drink.*]

GEORGE: Martha's going to put on some rhythm she understands . . . Sacre du Printemps, maybe. [*Moves . . . sits by* HONEY.] Hi, sexy.

HONEY [*a little giggle-scream*]: Oooooohhhhh!

GEORGE [*laughs mockingly*]: Ha, ha, ha, ha, ha. Choose it, Martha . . . do your stuff!

MARTHA [*concentrating on the machine*]: You're damn right!

GEORGE [*to* HONEY]: You want to dance with me, angel-tits?

NICK: What did you call my wife?

GEORGE [*derisively*]: Oh boy!

HONEY [*petulantly*]: No! If I can't do my interpretive dance, I don't want to dance with anyone. I'll just sit here and . . . [*Shrugs . . . drinks.*]

MARTHA [*record on . . . a jazzy slow pop tune*]: O.K. stuff, let's go. [*Grabs* NICK.]

NICK: Hm? Oh . . . hi.

MARTHA: Hi. [*They dance, close together, slowly.*]

HONEY [*pouting*]: We'll just sit here and watch.

GEORGE: That's *right!*

MARTHA [*to* NICK]: Hey, you *are* strong, aren't you?

NICK: Unh-hunh.

MARTHA: I like that.

NICK: Unh-hunh.

HONEY: They're dancing like they've danced before.

GEORGE: It's a familiar dance . . . they both know it. . . .

MARTHA: Don't be shy.

NICK: I'm . . . not. . . .

GEORGE [*to* HONEY]: It's a very old ritual, monkey-nipples
. . . old as they come.

HONEY: I . . . I don't know what you mean.

> [NICK *and* MARTHA *move apart now, and dance on
> either side of where* GEORGE *and* HONEY *are sitting;
> they face each other, and while their feet move but little,
> their bodies undulate congruently. . . . It is as if they were
> pressed together.*]

MARTHA: I like the way you move.

NICK: I like the way you move, too.

GEORGE [*to* HONEY]: They like the way they move.

HONEY [*not entirely with it*]: That's nice.

MARTHA [*to* NICK]: I'm surprised George didn't give you his
side of things.

GEORGE [*to* HONEY]: Aren't they cute?

NICK: Well, he didn't.

MARTHA: That surprises me.

> [*Perhaps* MARTHA's *statements are more or less in time
> to the music*]

NICK: Does it?

MARTHA: Yeah . . . he usually does . . . when he gets the
chance.

NICK: Well, what do you know.

MARTHA: It's really a very sad story.

GEORGE: You have ugly talents, Martha.

NICK: Is it?

MARTHA: It would make you weep.

GEORGE: Hideous gifts.

NICK: Is that so?

GEORGE: Don't encourage her.

MARTHA: Encourage me.

NICK: Go on.

[*They may undulate towards each other and then move back.*]

GEORGE: I warn you . . . don't encourage her.

MARTHA: He warns you . . . don't encourage me.

NICK: I heard him . . . tell me more.

MARTHA [*consciously making rhymed speech*]:
> Well, Georgie-boy had lots of big ambitions
> In spite of something funny in his past. . . .

GEORGE [*quietly warning*]: Martha . . .

MARTHA: Which Georgie-boy here turned into a novel. . . .
> His first attempt and also his last . . .
  Hey! I rhymed! I rhymed!

GEORGE: I warn you, Martha.

NICK: Yeah . . . you rhymed. Go on, go on.

MARTHA: But Daddy took a look at Georgie's novel . . .

GEORGE: You're looking for a punch in the mouth. . . . You know that, Martha.

MARTHA: Do tell! . . . and he was very shocked by what he read.

NICK: He was?

MARTHA: Yes . . . he was. . . . A novel all about a naughty boy-child . . .

GEORGE [*rising*]: I will not tolerate this!

NICK [*offhand, to* GEORGE]: Oh, can it.

MARTHA: . . . ha, ha!
> naughty boychild

who . . . uh . . . who killed his mother and his father
dead.

GEORGE: STOP IT, MARTHA!

MARTHA: And Daddy said . . . Look here, I will not let you
publish such a thing. . . .

GEORGE [*rushes to phonograph . . . rips the record off*]:
That's it! The dancing's over. That's it. Go on now!

NICK: What do you think you're doing, hunh?

HONEY [*happily*]: Violence! Violence!

MARTHA [*loud: a pronouncement*]: And Daddy said . . . Look
here, kid, you don't think for a second I'm going to let you
publish this crap, do you? Not on your life, baby . . . not
while you're teaching here. . . . You publish that goddamn
book and you're out . . . on your ass!

GEORGE: DESIST! DESIST!

MARTHA: Ha, ha, ha, HA!

NICK [*laughing*]: De . . . sist!

HONEY: Oh, violence . . . violence!

MARTHA: Why, the idea! A teacher at a respected, conser-
vative institution like this, in a town like New Carthage,
publishing a book like that? If you respect your position
here, young man, young . . . whippersnapper, you'll just
withdraw that manuscript. . . .

GEORGE: I will not be made mock of!

NICK: He will not be made mock of, for Christ's sake.
[*Laughs.*]

[HONEY *joins in the laughter, not knowing exactly
why.*]

GEORGE: I will not!

[*All three are laughing at him.*]

[*Infuriated*] THE GAME IS OVER!

MARTHA [*pushing on*]: Imagine such a thing! A book about
a boy who murders his mother and kills his father, and pre-
tends it's all an accident!

HONEY [*beside herself with glee*]: An accident!

NICK [*remembering something related*]: Hey . . . wait a
  minute . . .

MARTHA [*her own voice now*]: And you want to know the
  clincher? You want to know what big brave Georgie said
  to Daddy?

GEORGE: NO! NO! NO! NO!

NICK: Wait a minute now. . . .

MARTHA: Georgie said . . . but Daddy . . . I mean . . . ha, ha,
  ha, ha . . . but *Sir,* it isn't a *novel* at all. . . [*Other voice*] Not
  a novel? [*Mimicking* GEORGE's *voice*] No, sir. . . it isn't a
  novel at all. . . .

GEORGE [*advancing on her*]: You will not say this!

NICK [*sensing the danger*]: Hey.

MARTHA: The hell I won't. Keep away from me, you bastard!
  [*Backs off a little . . . uses* GEORGE's *voice again.*]
  No, Sir, this isn't a novel at all. . . this is the truth . . . this
  really happened. . . . TO ME!

GEORGE [*on her*]: I'LL KILL YOU!
  [*Grabs her by the throat. They struggle.*]

NICK: HEY! [*Comes between them.*]

HONEY [*wildly*]: VIOLENCE! VIOLENCE!
  [GEORGE, MARTHA, *and* NICK *struggle . . . yells, etc.*]

MARTHA: IT HAPPENED! TO ME! TO ME!

GEORGE: YOU SATANIC BITCH!

NICK: STOP THAT! STOP THAT!

HONEY: VIOLENCE! VIOLENCE!
  [*The other three struggle,* GEORGE's *hands are on*
  MARTHA's *throat,* NICK *grabs him, tears him from*
  MARTHA, *throws him on the floor.* GEORGE, *on the*
  floor; NICK *over him;* MARTHA *to one side, her hand on*
  her throat.]

NICK: That's enough now!

HONEY [*disappointment in her voice*]: Oh . . . oh . . . oh . . .
  [GEORGE *drags himself into a chair. He is hurt, but it is*
  more a profound humiliation than a physical injury.]

GEORGE [*they watch him . . . a pause . . .*]: All right. . . all right . . . very quiet now . . . we will all be . . . very quiet.

MARTHA [*softly, with a slow shaking of her head*]: Murderer. Mur . . . der . . . er.

NICK [*softly to* MARTHA]: O.K. now . . . that's enough.
[*A brief silence. They all move around a little, self-consciously, like wrestlers flexing after a fall.*]

GEORGE [*composure seemingly recovered, but there is a great nervous intensity*]: Well! That's one game. What shall we do now, hunh?
[MARTHA *and* NICK *laugh nervously.*]
Oh come on . . . let's think of something else. We've played Humiliate the Host. . . we've gone through that one . . . what shall we do now?

NICK: Aw . . . look. . . .

GEORGE: AW LOOK! [*Whines it*] Awww . . . looooook. [*Alert*] I mean, come on! We must know other games, college-type types like us . . . that can't be the . . . limit of our vocabulary, can it?

NICK: I think maybe . . .

GEORGE: Let's see now . . . what else can we do? There are other games. How about . . . how about . . . Hump the Hostess? HUNH?? How about that? How about Hump the Hostess? [*To* NICK] You wanna play that one? You wanna play Hump the Hostess? HUNH? HUNH?

NICK [*a little frightened*]: Calm down, now.
[MARTHA *giggles quietly.*]

GEORGE: Or is that for later . . . mount her like a goddamn dog?

HONEY [*wildly toasting everybody*]: Hump the Hostess!

NICK [*to* HONEY . . . *sharply*]: Just shut up . . . will you?
[HONEY *does, her glass in mid-air.*]

GEORGE: You don't wanna play that now, hunh? You wanna save that game till later? Well, what'll we play now? We gotta play a game.

MARTHA [*quietly*]: Portrait of a man drowning.

GEORGE [*affirmatively, but to none of them*]: I am not drowning.

HONEY [*to* NICK, *tearfully indignant*]: You told me to shut up!

NICK [*impatiently*]: I'm sorry.

HONEY [*between her teeth*]: No you're not.

NICK [*to* HONEY, *even more impatiently*]: I'm sorry.

GEORGE [*claps his hands together, once, loud*]: I've got it! I'll tell you what game we'll play. We're done with Humiliate the Host . . . this round, anyway . . . we're done with that . . . and we don't want to play Hump the Hostess, yet . . . not yet . . . so I know what we'll play. . . . We'll play a round of Get the Guests. How about that? How about a little game of Get the Guests?

MARTHA [*turning away, a little disgusted*]: Jesus, George.

GEORGE: Book dropper! Child mentioner!

HONEY: I don't like these games.

NICK: Yeah. . . . I think maybe we've had enough of games, now. . . .

GEORGE: Oh, no . . . oh, no . . . we haven't. We've had only one game. . . . Now we're going to have another. You can't fly on one game.

NICK: I think maybe . . .

GEORGE [*with great authority*]: SILENCE! [*It is respected.*] Now, how are we going to play Get the Guests?

MARTHA: For God's sake, George. . . .

GEORGE: You be quiet!

[MARTHA *shrugs.*]

I wonder. . . . I wonder. [*Puzzles . . . then . . .*] O.K.! Well . . . Martha . . . in her indiscreet way . . . well, not really indiscreet, because Martha is a naïve, at heart. . . anyway, Martha told you all about my first novel. True or false? Hunh? I mean, true or false that there ever was such a thing. HA! But, Martha told you about it . . . my first novel, my . . . memory book . . . which I'd sort of preferred she hadn't, but hell, that's blood under the bridge. BUT! what she didn't do . . . what Martha didn't tell you about is she didn't tell us all about my *second* novel.

[MARTHA *looks at him with puzzled curiosity.*]

No, you didn't know about that, did you, Martha? About my second novel, true or false. True or false?

MARTHA [*sincerely*]: No.

GEORGE: No.

[*He starts quietly but as he goes on his tone becomes harsher, his voice louder.*]

Well, it's an allegory, really – probably – but it can be read as straight, cosy prose . . . and it's all about a nice young couple who come out of the middle-west. It's a bucolic, you see. AND, this nice young couple comes out of the middle-west, and he's blond and about thirty, and he's a scientist, a teacher, a scientist. . . and his mouse is a wifey little type who gargles brandy all the time . . . and . . .

NICK: Just a minute here. . . .

GEORGE: . . . and they got to know each other when they was only teensie little types, and they used to get under the vanity table and poke around, and . . .

NICK: I said JUST A MINUTE!

GEORGE: This is my game! You played yours . . . you people. This is my game!

HONEY [*dreamy*]: I want to hear the story. I love stories.

MARTHA: George, for heaven's sake. . . .

GEORGE: AND! And Mousie's father was a holy man, see, and he ran sort of a travelling clip joint, based on Christ and all those girls, and he took the faithful . . . that's all . . . just took 'em. . . .

HONEY [*puzzling*]: This is familiar. . . .

NICK [*voice shaking a little*]: No kidding!

GEORGE: . . . and he died eventually, Mousie's pa, and they pried him open, and all sorts of money fell out. . . . Jesus money, Mary money. . . . LOOT!

HONEY [*dreamy, puzzling*]: I've heard this story before.

NICK [*with quiet intensity . . . to waken her*]: Honey. . . .

GEORGE: But that's in the backwash, in the early part of the book. Anyway, Blondie and his frau out of the plain states came. [*Chuckles.*]

MARTHA: Very funny, George. . . .

GEORGE: . . . thank you . . . and settled in a town just like nouveau Carthage here. . . .

NICK [*threatening*]: I don't think you'd better go on, mister. . . .

GEORGE: Do you not!

NICK [*less certainly*]: No. I . . . I don't think you'd better.

HONEY: I love familiar stories . . . they're the best.

GEORGE: How right you are. But Blondie was in disguise, really, all got up as a teacher, 'cause his baggage ticket had bigger things writ on it. . . H.I. HI! Historical inevitability.

NICK: There's no need for you to go any further, now. . . .

HONEY [*puzzling to make sense out of what she is hearing*]: Let them go on.

GEORGE: We shall. And he had this baggage with him, and part of this baggage was in the form of his mouse. . . .

NICK: We don't have to listen to this!

HONEY: Why not?

GEORGE: Your bride has a point. And one of the things nobody could understand about Blondie was his baggage . . . his mouse, I mean, here he was, pan-Kansas swimming champeen, or something, and he had this mouse, of whom he was solicitous to a point that faileth human understanding . . . given that she was sort of a simp, in the long run. . . .

NICK: This isn't fair of you. . . .

GEORGE: Perhaps not. Like, as I said, his mouse, she tooted brandy immodestly and spent half of her time in the upchuck. . . .

HONEY [*focusing*]: I know these people. . . .

GEORGE: Do you! . . . But she was a money baggage amongst other things . . . Godly money ripped from the golden teeth of the unfaithful, a pragmatic extension of the big dream . . . and she was put up with. . . .

HONEY [*some terror*]: I don't like this story. . . .

NICK [*surprisingly pleading*]: Please . . . please don't.

MARTHA: Maybe you better stop, George. . . .

GEORGE: . . . and she was put up with. . . . STOP? Ha-ha.

NICK: Please . . . please don't.

GEORGE: Beg, baby.

MARTHA: George. . . .

GEORGE: . . . and . . . oh, we get a flashback here, to How They Got Married.

NICK: NO!

GEORGE [*triumphant*]: YES!

NICK [*almost whining*]: Why?

GEORGE: How They Got Married. Well, how they got married is this. . . . The Mouse got all puffed up one day, and she went over to Blondie's house, and she stuck out her puff, and she said . . . look at me.

HONEY [*white . . . on her feet*]: I . . . don't. . . like this.

NICK [*to* GEORGE]: Stop it!

GEORGE: Look at me . . . I'm all puffed up. Oh my goodness, said Blondie. . . .

HONEY [*as from a distance*] :. . . and so they were married . . .

GEORGE: . . . and so they were married. . . .

HONEY: . . . and then . . .

GEORGE: . . . and then . . .

HONEY [*hysteria*]: WHAT? . . . and then, WHAT?

NICK: NO! No!

GEORGE [*as if to a baby*]: . . . and then the puff went *away* . . . like magic . . . pouf !

NICK [*almost sick*]: Jesus God. . . .

HONEY: . . . the puff went away. . . .

GEORGE [*softly*]: . . . pouf.

NICK: Honey . . . I didn't mean to . . . honestly, I didn't mean to . . .

HONEY: You . . . you told them. . . .

NICK: Honey . . . I didn't mean to. . . .

HONEY [*with outlandish horror*]: You . . . told them! You told them! OOOOHHHH! Oh, no, no, no, no! You couldn't have told them . . . oh, noooo!

NICK: Honey, I didn't mean to. . . .

HONEY [*grabbing at her belly*]: Ohhhhh . . . nooooo.

NICK: Honey . . . baby . . . I'm sorry . . . I didn't mean to. . . .

GEORGE [*abruptly and with some disgust*]: And that's how you play Get the Guests.

HONEY: I'm going to . . . I'm going to be . . . sick. . . .

GEORGE: Naturally!

NICK: Honey. . . .

HONEY [*hysterical*]: Leave me alone . . . I'm going . . . to . . . be . . . sick.

[*She runs out of the room.*]

MARTHA [*shaking her head, watching* HONEY's *retreating form*]: God Almighty.

GEORGE [*shrugging*]: The patterns of history.

NICK [*quietly shaking*]: You shouldn't have done that. . . you shouldn't have done that at all.

GEORGE [*calmly*]: I hate hypocrisy.

NICK: That was cruel. . . and vicious . . .

GEORGE: . . . she'll get over it. . . .

NICK: . . . and damaging . . . !

GEORGE: . . . she'll recover. . . .

NICK: DAMAGING!! TO ME!!

GEORGE [*with wonder*]: To you!

NICK: TO ME!!

GEORGE: To you!!

NICK: YES!!

GEORGE: Oh beautiful . . . beautiful. By God, you gotta have a swine to show you where the truffles are. [*So calmly*] Well, you just rearrange your alliances, boy. You just pick up the pieces where you can . . . you just look around and make the best of things . . . you scramble back up on your feet.

MARTHA [*quietly, to* NICK]: Go look after your wife.

GEORGE: Yeah . . . go pick up the pieces and plan some new strategy.

NICK [*to* GEORGE, *as he moves towards the hall*]: You're going to regret this.

GEORGE: Probably. I regret everything.

NICK: I mean, I'm going to make you regret this.

GEORGE [*softly*]: No doubt. Acute embarrassment, eh?

NICK: I'll play the charades like you've got 'em set up. . . . I'll play in your language. . . . I'll be what you say I am.

GEORGE: You are already . . . you just don't know it.

NICK [*shaking within*]: No . . . no. Not really. But I'll *be* it, mister. . . . I'll show you something come to life you'll wish you hadn't set up.

GEORGE: Go clean up the mess.

NICK [*quietly . . . intensely*]: You just wait, mister.

[*He exits. Pause,* GEORGE *smiles at* MARTHA.]

MARTHA: Very good, George.

GEORGE: Thank you, Martha.

MARTHA: Really good.

GEORGE: I'm glad you liked it.

MARTHA: I mean . . . You did a good job . . . you really fixed it.

GEORGE: Unh-hunh.

MARTHA: It's the most. . . life you've shown in a long time.

GEORGE: You bring out the best in me, baby.

MARTHA: Yeah . . . pigmy hunting!

GEORGE: PIGMY!

MARTHA: You're really a bastard.

GEORGE: I? I?

MARTHA: Yeah . . . you.

GEORGE: Baby, if quarterback there is a pigmy, you've certainly changed your style. What are you after now . . . giants?

MARTHA: You make me sick.

GEORGE: It's perfectly all right for you. . . . I mean, you can make your own rules . . . you can go around like a hopped-up Arab, slashing away at everything in sight, scarring up half the world if you want to. But somebody else try it. . . no sir!

MARTHA: You miserable . . .

GEORGE [*mocking*]: Why baby, I did it all for you. I thought you'd like it, sweetheart. . . it's sort of to your taste . . . blood, carnage, and all. Why, I thought you'd get all excited . . . sort of heave and pant and come running at me, your melons bobbling.

MARTHA: You've really screwed up, George.

GEORGE [*spitting it out*]: Oh, for God's sake, Martha!

MARTHA: I mean it . . . you really have.

GEORGE [*barely contained anger now*]: You can sit there in that chair of yours, you can sit there with the gin running out of your mouth, and you can humiliate me, you can tear me apart. . . ALL NIGHT . . . and that's perfectly all right. . . that's O.K. . . .

MARTHA: YOU CAN STAND IT!

GEORGE: I CANNOT STAND IT!!

MARTHA: YOU CAN STAND IT! YOU MARRIED ME FOR IT!!
    [*A silence.*]

GEORGE [*quietly*]: That is a desperately sick lie.

MARTHA: DON'T YOU KNOW IT, EVEN YET?

GEORGE [*shaking his head*]: Oh . . . Martha.

MARTHA: My arm has gotten tired whipping you.

GEORGE [*stares at her in disbelief*]: You're mad.

MARTHA: For twenty-three years!

GEORGE: You're deluded . . . Martha, you're deluded.

MARTHA: IT'S NOT WHAT I'VE WANTED!

GEORGE: I thought at least you were . . . on to yourself. I didn't know. I . . . didn't know.

MARTHA [*anger taking over*]: I'm on to myself.

GEORGE [*as if she were some sort of bug*]: No . . . no . . . you're . . . sick.

MARTHA [*rises – screams*]: I'LL SHOW YOU WHO'S SICK!

GEORGE: All right, Martha . . . you're going too far.

MARTHA [*screams again*]: I'LL SHOW YOU WHO'S SICK, I'LL SHOW YOU.

GEORGE [*he shakes her*]: Stop it! [*Pushes her back in her chair.*] Now, stop it!

MARTHA [*calmer*]: I'll show you who's sick. [*Calmer*] Boy, you're really having a field day, hunh? Well, I'm going to finish you . . . before I'm through with you. . . .

GEORGE: . . . you and the quarterback . . . you both gonna finish me . . . ?

MARTHA: . . . before I'm through with you you'll wish you'd died in that automobile, you bastard.

GEORGE [*emphasizing with his forefinger*]: And you'll wish you'd never mentioned our son!

MARTHA [*dripping contempt*]: You . . .

GEORGE: Now, I said I warned you.

MARTHA: I'm impressed.

GEORGE: I warned you not to go too far.

MARTHA: I'm just beginning.

GEORGE [*calmly, matter-of-factly*]: I'm numbed enough . . . and I don't mean by liquor, though maybe that's been part of the process – a gradual, over-the-years going to sleep of the brain cells – I'm numbed enough, now, to be able to take you when we're alone. I don't listen to you . . . or when I *do* listen to you, I sift everything, I bring everything down to reflex response, so I don't really *hear* you, which is the only way to manage it. But you've taken a new tack, Martha, over the past couple of centuries – or however long it's been I've lived in this house with you – that makes it just too much . . . too much. I don't mind your dirty underthings in public . . . well, I *do* mind, but I've reconciled myself to that . . . but you've moved bag and baggage into your own fantasy world now, and you've started playing variations on your own distortions, and, as a result . . .

MARTHA: Nuts!

GEORGE: Yes . . . you have.

MARTHA: Nuts!

GEORGE: Well, you can go on like that as long as you want to. And, when you're done . . .

MARTHA: Have you ever listened to your sentences, George? Have you ever listened to the way you talk? You're so frigging . . . convoluted . . . that's what you are. You talk like you were writing one of your stupid papers.

GEORGE: Actually, I'm rather worried about you. About your mind.

MARTHA: Don't you worry about my mind, sweetheart!

GEORGE: I think I'll have you committed.

MARTHA : YOU WHAT?

GEORGE [*quietly . . . distinctly*]: I think I'll have you committed.

MARTHA [*breaks into long laughter*]: Oh baby, aren't you something!

GEORGE: I've got to find some way to really get at you.

MARTHA: You've got at me, George . . . you don't have to do anything. Twenty-three years of you has been quite enough.

GEORGE: Will you go quietly, then?

MARTHA: You know what's happened, George? You want to know what's *really happened*? [*Snaps her fingers.*] It's snapped, finally. Not me . . . *it*. The whole arrangement. You can go along . . . forever, and everything's . . . manageable. You make all sorts of excuses to yourself . . .

you know . . . this is life . . . the hell with it. . . maybe
tomorrow he'll be dead . . . maybe tomorrow *you'll* be dead
. . . all sorts of excuses. But then, one day, one night, something happens . . . and SNAP! It breaks. And you just don't
give a damn any more. I've tried with you, baby . . . really,
I've tried.

GEORGE: Come off it, Martha.

MARTHA: I've tried . . . I've really tried.

GEORGE [*with some awe*]: You're a monster . . . you *are*.

MARTHA: I'm loud, and I'm vulgar, and I wear the pants in
this house because somebody's got to, but I am *not* a
monster. I am *not*.

GEORGE: You're a spoiled, self-indulgent, wilful, dirty-
minded, liquor-ridden . . .

MARTHA: SNAP! It went snap. Look, I'm not going to try to
get through to you any more. . . . I'm not going to try.
There was a second back there, maybe, there was a second,
just a second, when I could have gotten through to you,
when maybe we could have cut through all this crap. But
that's past, and now I'm not going to try.

GEORGE: Once a month, Martha! I've gotten used to it . . .
once a month and we get misunderstood Martha, the good-
hearted girl underneath the barnacles, the little Miss that
the touch of kindness'd bring to bloom again. And I've
believed it more times than I want to remember, because I
don't want to think I'm that much of a sucker. I don't
believe you . . . I just don't believe you. There is no moment
. . . there is no moment any more when we could . . . come
together.

MARTHA [*armed again*]: Well, maybe you're right, baby. You
can't come together with nothing, and you're nothing!
SNAP! It went snap tonight at Daddy's party. [*Dripping
contempt, but there is fury and loss under it.*] I sat there at
Daddy's party, and I watched you . . . I watched you sitting
there, and I watched the younger men around you, the men

who were going to go somewhere. And I sat there and I
watched you, and *you* weren't *there*! And it snapped! It
finally snapped! And I'm going to howl it out, and I'm not
going to give a damn what I do, and I'm going to make the
damned biggest explosion you ever heard.

GEORGE [*very pointedly*]: You try it and I'll beat you at your
own game.

MARTHA [*hopefully*]: Is that a threat, George? Hunh?

GEORGE: That's a threat, Martha.

MARTHA [*fake-spits at him*]: You're going to get it, baby.

GEORGE: Be careful, Martha . . . I'll rip you to pieces.

MARTHA: You aren't man enough . . . you haven't got the
guts.

GEORGE: Total war?

MARTHA : Total.

   [*Silence. They both seem relieved . . . elated,* NICK *re-
   enters.*]

NICK [*brushing his hands off*]: Well . . . she's . . . resting.

GEORGE [*quietly amused at* NICK's *calm, off-hand manner*]:
Oh?

MARTHA: Yeah? She all right?

NICK: I think so . . . now. I'm . . . terribly sorry. . . .

MARTHA: Forget about it.

GEORGE: Happens all the time around here.

NICK: She'll be all right.

MARTHA: She lying down? You put her upstairs? On a bed?

NICK [*making himself a drink*]: Well, no, actually. Uh . . . may
I? She's . . . in the bathroom. . . on the bathroom floor . . .
she's lying there.

GEORGE [*considers it*]: Well . . . that's not very nice.

NICK: She likes it. She says it's . . . cool.

GEORGE: Still, I don't think. . . .

MARTHA [*overruling him*]: If she wants to lie on the
bathroom floor, let her. [*To* NICK, *seriously*] Maybe she'd
be more comfortable in the tub?

NICK [*he, too, seriously*]: No, she says she likes the floor . . . she took up the mat, and she's lying on the tiles. She . . . she lies on the floor a lot . . . she really does.

MARTHA [*pause*]: Oh.

NICK: She . . . she gets lots of headaches and things, and she always lies on the floor. [*To* GEORGE] Is there . . . ice?

GEORGE: What?

NICK: Ice. Is there ice?

GEORGE [*as if the word were unfamiliar to him*]: Ice?

NICK: Ice. Yes.

MARTHA: Ice.

GEORGE [*as if he suddenly understood*]: Ice!

MARTHA: Attaboy.

GEORGE [*without moving*]: Oh, yes . . . I'll get some.

MARTHA: Well, go. [*Mugging . . . to* NICK] Besides, we want to be alone.

GEORGE [*moving to take the bucket*]: I wouldn't be surprised, Martha . . . I wouldn't be surprised.

MARTHA [*as if insulted*]: Oh, you wouldn't, hunh?

GEORGE: Not a bit, Martha.

MARTHA [*violent*]: NO?

GEORGE [*he too*]: NO! [*Quietly again*] You'll try anything, Martha.

[*Picks up the ice bucket.*]

NICK [*to cover*]: Actually, she's very . . . frail, and . . .

GEORGE: . . . slim-hipped.

NICK [*remembering*]: Yes . . . exactly.

GEORGE [*at the hallway . . . not kindly*]: That why you don't have any kids?

[*He exits.*]

NICK [*to* GEORGE's *retreating form*]: Well, I don't know that that's . . . [*Trails off*] . . . if that has anything to do with any . . . thing.

MARTHA: Well, if it does, who cares? Hunh?

NICK: Pardon?

[MARTHA *blows him a kiss.*]

NICK [*still concerned with* GEORGE's *remark*]: I . . . what?
. . . I'm sorry.

MARTHA: I said . . . [*Blows him another kiss.*]

NICK [*uncomfortable*]: Oh . . . yes.

MARTHA: Hey . . . hand me a cigarette . . . lover. [NICK *fishes
in his pocket.*] That's a good boy. [*He gives her one.*] Unh
. . . thanks.

[*He lights it for her. As he does, she slips her hand
between his legs, somewhere between the knee and the
crotch, bringing her hand around to the outside of his
leg.*]

Ummmmmmmrnrn.

[*He seems uncertain, but does not move. She smiles,
moves her hand a little.*]

Now, for being such a good boy, you can give me a kiss.
C'mon.

NICK [*nervously*]: Look . . . I don't think we should. . . .

MARTHA: C'mon, baby . . . a friendly kiss.

NICK [*still uncertain*]: Well. . . .

MARTHA: . . . you won't get hurt, little boy. . . .

NICK: . . . not so little. . . .

MARTHA: I'll bet you're not. C'mon. . . .

NICK [*weakening*]: But what if he should come back in, and
. . . or . . . ?

MARTHA [*all the while her hand is moving up and down his
leg*]: George? Don't worry about him. Besides, who could
object to a friendly little kiss? It's all in the faculty.

[*They both laugh, quietly . . .* NICK *a little nervously.*]

We're a close-knit family here . . . Daddy always says so.
. . . Daddy wants us to get to know each other . . . that's
what he had the party for tonight. So c'mon . . . let's get to
know each other a little bit.

NICK: It isn't that I don't want to . . . believe me. . . .

MARTHA: You're a scientist, aren't you? C'mon . . . make an

experiment . . . make a little experiment. Experiment on old Martha.

NICK [*giving in*]: . . . not very old. . . .

MARTHA: That's right, not very old, but lots of good experience . . . lots of it.

NICK: I'll. . . I'll bet.

MARTHA [*as they draw slowly closer*]: It'll be a nice change for you, too.

NICK: Yes, it would.

MARTHA: And you could go back to your little wife all refreshed.

NICK [*closer . . . almost whispering*]: She wouldn't know the difference.

MARTHA: Well, nobody else's going to know, either.

[*They come together. What might have been a joke rapidly becomes serious, with* MARTHA *urging it in that direction. There is no frenetic quality, but rather a slow, continually involving intertwining. Perhaps* MARTHA *is still more or less in her chair, and* NICK *is sort of beside and on the chair.*

GEORGE *enters . . . stops . . . watches a moment . . . smiles . . . laughs silently, nods his head, turns, exits, without being noticed.*

NICK, *who has already had his hand on* MARTHA's *breast, now puts his hand inside her dress.*]

MARTHA [*slowing him down*]: Hey . . . hey. Take it easy, boy. Down, baby. Don't rush it, hunh?

NICK [*his eyes still closed*]: Oh, c'mon, now. . . .

MARTHA [*pushing him away*]: Unh-hunh. Later, baby . . . later.

NICK: I told you . . . I'm a biologist.

MARTHA [*soothing him*]: I know. I can tell. Later, hunh?

[GEORGE *is heard off-stage, singing 'Who's afraid of Virginia Woolf?'* MARTHA *and* NICK *go apart,* NICK *wiping his mouth,* MARTHA *checking her clothes. Safely later,* GEORGE *re-enters with the ice bucket.*]

GEORGE: . . . of Virginia Woolf,
                Virginia Woolf,
                Virginia . . .

. . . ah! Here we are . . . ice for the lamps of China, Manchuria thrown in. [*To* NICK] You better watch those yellow bastards, my love . . . they aren't amused. Why don't you come on over to our side, and we'll blow the hell out of 'em. Then we can split up the money between us and be on Easy Street. What d'ya say?

NICK [*not at all sure what is being talked about*]: Well . . . sure. Hey! Ice!

GEORGE [*with hideously false enthusiasm*]: Right! [*Now to* MARTHA, *purring*] Hello, Martha . . . my dove. . . . You look . . . radiant.

MARTHA [*off-hand*]: Thank you.

GEORGE [*very cheerful*]: Well now, let me see. I've got the ice . . .

MARTHA: . . . gotten. . . .

GEORGE: *Got,* Martha. Got is perfectly correct . . . it's just a little . . . archaic, like you.

MARTHA [*suspicious*]: What are you so cheerful about?

GEORGE [*ignoring the remark*]: Let's see now . . . I've got the ice. Can I make someone a drink? Martha, can I make you a drink?

MARTHA [*bravura*]: Yeah, why not?

GEORGE [*taking her glass*]: Indeed . . . why not? [*Examines the glass.*] Martha! You've been nibbling away at the glass.

MARTHA: I have not!

GEORGE [*to* NICK, *who is at the bar*]: I see you're making your own, which is fine . . . fine. I'll just hootch up Martha, here, and then we'll be all set.

MARTHA [*suspicious*]: All set for what?

GEORGE [*pause . . . considers*]: Why, I don't know. We're having a party, aren't we? [*To* NICK, *who has moved from the bar*] I passed your wife in the hall. I mean, I passed the john and I looked in on her. Peaceful. . . so peaceful. Sound asleep . . . and she's actually . . . sucking her thumb.

MARTHA: Awwwwww!

GEORGE: Rolled up like a foetus, sucking away.

NICK [*a little uncomfortably*]: I suppose she's all right.

GEORGE [*expansively*]: Of course she is! [*Hands* MARTHA *her drink.*] There you are.

MARTHA [*still on her guard*]: Thanks.

GEORGE: And now one for me. It's my turn.

MARTHA: Never, baby . . . it's never your turn.

GEORGE [*too cheerful*]: Oh, now, I wouldn't say that, Martha.

MARTHA: You moving on the principle the worm turns? Well, the worm part's O.K. . . . 'cause that fits you fine, but the turning part . . . unh-unh! You're in a straight line, buddy-boy, and it doesn't lead anywhere . . . [*A vague afterthought.*] . . . except maybe the grave.

GEORGE [*chuckles, takes his drink*]: Well, you just hold that thought, Martha . . . hug it close . . . run your hands over it. Me, I'm going to sit down . . . if you'll excuse me. . . . I'm going to sit down over there and read a book.

[*He moves to a chair facing away from the centre of the room, but not too far from the front door.*]

MARTHA: You're gonna do *what*?

GEORGE [*quietly, distinctly*]: I am going to read a book. Read. Read. Read? You've heard of it? [*Picks up a book.*]

MARTHA [*standing*]: Whaddya mean you're gonna read? What's the matter with you?

GEORGE [*too calmly*]: There's nothing the matter with me, Martha. . . . I'm going to read a book. That's all.

MARTHA [*oddly furious*]: We've got company!

GEORGE [*over-patiently*]: I know, my dear. . . [*Looks at his watch.*] . . . but. . . it's after four o'clock, and I always read around this time. Now, you . . . [*Dismisses her with a little*

wave] . . . go about your business. . . . I'll sit here very
quietly. . . .

MARTHA: You read in the afternoon! You read at four
o'clock in the afternoon . . . you don't read at four o'clock
in the morning! Nobody reads at four o'clock in the
morning!

GEORGE [*absorbing himself in his book*]: Now, now, now.

MARTHA [*incredulously, to* NICK]: He's going to read a
book. . . . The son of a bitch is going to read a book!

NICK [*smiling a little*]: So it would seem.

[*Moves to* MARTHA, *puts his arm around her waist.*
GEORGE *cannot see this, of course.*]

MARTHA [*getting an idea*]: Well, we can amuse ourselves,
can't we?

NICK: I imagine so.

MARTHA: We're going to amuse ourselves, George.

GEORGE [*not looking up*]: Unh-hunh. That's nice.

MARTHA: You might not like it.

GEORGE [*never looking up*]: No, no, now . . . you go right
ahead . . . you entertain your guests.

MARTHA: I'm going to entertain myself, too.

GEORGE: Good . . . good.

MARTHA: Ha, ha. You're a riot, George.

GEORGE: Unh-hunh.

MARTHA: Well, I'm a riot, too, George.

GEORGE: Yes, you are, Martha.

[NICK *takes* MARTHA's *hand, pulls her to him. They stop
for a moment, then kiss, not briefly.*]

MARTHA [*after*]: You know what I'm doing, George?

GEORGE: No, Martha . . . what are you doing?

MARTHA: I'm entertaining. I'm entertaining one of the guests.
I'm necking with one of the guests.

GEORGE [*seemingly relaxed and preoccupied, never looking*]:
Oh, that's nice. Which one?

MARTHA [*livid*]: Oh, by God, you're funny. [*Breaks away*

from NICK . . . *moves into* GEORGE's *side-line of vision by herself. Her balance is none too good, and she bumps into or brushes against the door chimes by the door. They chime.*]

GEORGE: Someone at the door, Martha.

MARTHA: Never mind that. I said I was necking with one of the guests.

GEORGE: Good . . . good. You go right on.

MARTHA [*pauses . . . not knowing quite what to do*]: Good?

GEORGE: Yes, good . . . good for you.

MARTHA [*her eyes narrowing, her voice becoming hard*]: Oh, I see what you're up to, you lousy little . . .

GEORGE: I'm up to page a hundred and . . .

MARTHA Cut it! Just cut it out! [*She hits against the door chimes again; they chime.*] Goddamn bongs.

GEORGE: They're chimes, Martha. Why don't you go back to your necking and stop bothering me? I want to read.

MARTHA: Why, you miserable. . . . I'll show *you*.

GEORGE [*swings around to face her . . . says, with great loathing*]: No . . . show him, Martha . . . he hasn't seen it. *Maybe* he hasn't seen it. [*Turns to* NICK.] You haven't seen it yet, have you?

NICK [*turning away, a look of disgust on his face*]: I . . . I have no respect for you.

GEORGE: And none for yourself, either. . . . [*Indicating* MARTHA] I don't know what the younger generation's coming to.

NICK: You don't. . . you don't even . . .

GEORGE: Care? You're quite right. . . . I couldn't care less. So, you just take this bag of laundry here, throw her over your shoulder, and . . .

NICK: You're disgusting.

GEORGE [*incredulous*]: *Because you're* going to hump Martha, *I'm* disgusting?

[*He breaks down in ridiculing laughter.*]

MARTHA [*to* GEORGE]: You Mother! [*To* NICK] Go wait for
me, hunh? Go wait for me in the kitchen. [*But* NICK *does
not move.* MARTHA *goes to him, puts her arms around
him.*] C'mon, baby . . . please. Wait for me . . . in the
kitchen . . . be a good baby.

    [NICK *takes her kiss, glares at* GEORGE . . . *who has
turned his back again . . . and exits.*

      MARTHA *swings around to* GEORGE.]

Now you listen to me. . . .

GEORGE: I'd rather read, Martha, if you don't mind. . . .

MARTHA [*her anger has her close to tears, her frustration to
fury*]: Well, I do mind. Now, you pay attention to me! You
come off this kick you're on, or I swear to God I'll do it. I
swear to God I'll follow that guy into the kitchen, and then
I'll take him upstairs, and . . .

GEORGE [*swinging around to her again . . . loud . . . loathing*]:
SO WHAT, MARTHA?

MARTHA [*considers him for a moment . . . then, nodding her
head, backing off slowly*]: O.K. . . . O.K. . . . You asked for
it . . . and you're going to get it.

GEORGE [*softly, sadly*]: Lord, Martha, if you want the boy
that much . . . have him . . . but do it honestly, will you?
Don't cover it over with all this . . . all this . . . footwork.

MARTHA [*hopeless*]: I'll make you sorry you made me want
to marry you. [*At the hallway*] I'll make you regret the day
you ever decided to come to this college. I'll make you sorry
you ever let yourself down.

    [*She exits.*

    Silence, GEORGE *sits still, staring straight ahead.
Listening . . . but there is no sound. Outwardly calm, he
returns to his book, reads a moment, then looks up . . .
considers. . . .*]

GEORGE: 'And the west, encumbered by crippling alliances,
and burdened with a morality too rigid to accommodate
itself to the swing of events, must. . . eventually . . . fall.'

[*He laughs, briefly, ruefully . . . rises, with the book in his hand. He stands still . . . then, quickly, he gathers all the fury he has been containing within himself . . . he shakes . . . he looks at the book in his hand and, with a cry that is part growl, part howl, he hurls it at the chimes. They crash against one another, ringing wildly. A brief pause, then* HONEY *enters.*]

HONEY [*the worse for wear, half asleep, still sick, weak, still staggering a little . . . vaguely, in something of a dream world*]: Bells. Ringing. I've been hearing bells.

GEORGE: Jesus!

HONEY: I couldn't sleep . . . for the bells. Ding-ding, bong . . . it woke me up. What time is it?

GEORGE [*quietly beside himself*]: Don't bother me.

HONEY [*confused and frightened*]: I was asleep, and the bells started . . . they BOOMED! Poe-bells . . . they were Poe-bells . . . Bing-bing-bong-BOOM!

GEORGE: BOOM!

HONEY: I was asleep, and I was dreaming of . . . something . . . and I heard the sounds coming, and I didn't know what it was.

GEORGE [*never quite to her*]: It was the sound of bodies. . . .

HONEY: And I didn't want to wake up, but the sound kept coming. . . .

GEORGE: . . . go back to sleep. . . .

HONEY: . . . and it FRIGHTENED ME!

GEORGE [*quietly . . . to* MARTHA, *as if she were in the room*]: I'm going to get you . . . Martha.

HONEY: And it was so . . . cold. The wind was . . . the wind was so cold! And I was lying somewhere, and the covers kept slipping away from me, and I didn't want them to . . .

GEORGE: Somehow, Martha.

HONEY: . . . and there was someone there . . . !

GEORGE: There was no one there.

HONEY [*frightened*]: And I didn't want someone there. . . . I was . . . naked . . . !

GEORGE: You don't know what's going on, do you?

HONEY [*still with her dream*]: I DON'T WANT ANY . . . NO . . . !

GEORGE: You don't know what's been going on around here while you been having your snoozette, do you?

HONEY: NO! . . . I DON'T WANT ANY . . . I DON'T WANT THEM. . . . GO 'WAY. . . . [*Begins to cry*] I DON'T WANT . . . ANY . . . CHILDREN. . . . I . . . don't. . . want . . . any . . . children. I'm afraid! I don't want to be hurt. . . . PLEASE!

GEORGE [*nodding his head. . . speaks with compassion*]: I should have known.

HONEY [*snapping awake from her reverie*]: What! What?

GEORGE: I should have known . . . the whole business . . . the headaches . . . the whining . . . the . . .

HONEY [*terrified*]: What are you talking about?

GEORGE [*ugly again*]: Does *he* know that? Does that . . . stud you're married to know about that, hunh?

HONEY: About what? Stay away from me!

GEORGE: Don't worry, baby . . . I wouldn't. . . . Oh, my God, that *would* be a joke, wouldn't it! But don't worry, baby, HEY! How you do it? Hunh? How do you make your secret little murders stud-boy doesn't know about, hunh? Pills? PILLS? You got a secret supply of pills? Or what? Apple jelly? WILL POWER?

HONEY: I feel sick.

GEORGE: You going to throw up again? You going to lie down on the cold tiles, your knees pulled up under your chin, your thumb stuck in your mouth . . . ?

HONEY [*panicked*]: Where is he?

GEORGE: Where's who? There's nobody here, baby.

HONEY: I want my husband! I want a drink!

GEORGE: Well, you just crawl over to the bar and make yourself one.

[*From off-stage comes the sound of* MARTHA's *laughter and the crashing of dishes.*]

[*Yelling*] That's right! Go at it!

HONEY: I want. . . something. . . .

GEORGE: You know what's going on in there, little Miss? Hunh? You hear all that? You know what's going on in there?

HONEY: I don't want to know anything!

GEORGE: There are a couple of people in there. . . .

[MARTHA's *laughter again.*]

. . . they are in there, in the kitchen. . . . Right there, with the onion skins and the coffee grounds . . . sort of . . . sort of a . . . sort of a dry run for the wave of the future.

HONEY [*beside herself*]: I . . . don't. . . understand . . . you. . . .

GEORGE [*a hideous elation*]: It's very simple. . . . When people can't abide things as they are, when they can't abide the present, they do one of two things . . . either they . . . either they turn to a contemplation of the past, as I have done, or they set about to . . . alter the future. And when you want to change something . . . you BANG! BANG! BANG! BANG!

HONEY: Stop it!

GEORGE: And you, you simpering bitch . . . you don't want *children*?

HONEY: You leave me . . . alone. Who . . . WHO RANG?

GEORGE: What?

HONEY: What were the bells? Who rang?

GEORGE: You don't want to know, do you? You don't want to listen to it, hunh?

HONEY [*shivering*]: I don't want to listen to you. . . . I want to know who rang.

GEORGE: Your husband is . . . and you want to know who *rang*?

HONEY: Who rang? Someone rang!

GEORGE [*his jaw drops open . . . he is whirling with an idea*]:
. . . Someone . . .

HONEY: RANG!

GEORGE: . . . someone . . . rang . . . yes . . . yessss. . . .

HONEY: The . . . bells . . . rang. . . .

GEORGE [*his mind racing ahead*]: The bells rang . . . and it
was someone . . .

HONEY: Somebody. . . .

GEORGE [*he is home, now*]: . . . somebody rang . . . it was
somebody . . . with . . . I'VE GOT IT! I'VE GOT IT,
MARTHA . . .! Somebody with a message . . . and the
message was . . . our son . . . OUR SON! [*Almost whispered*]
It was a message. . . the bells rang and it was a message,
and it was about. . . our son . . . and the message . . . was
. . . and the message was . . . our . . . son . . . is . . .
DEAD!

HONEY [*almost sick*]: Oh . . . no.

GEORGE [*cementing it in his mind*]: Our son is . . . dead. . . .
And . . . Martha doesn't know. . . . I haven't told . . .
Martha.

HONEY: No . . . no . . . no.

GEORGE [*slowly, deliberately*]: Our son is dead, and Martha
doesn't know.

HONEY: Oh. God in heaven . . . no.

GEORGE [*to* HONEY . . . *slowly, deliberately, dispassionately*]: And you're not going to tell her.

HONEY [*in tears*]: Your son is dead.

GEORGE: I'll tell her myself. . . in good time. I'll tell her
myself.

HONEY [*so faintly*]: I'm going to be sick.

GEORGE [*turning away from her . . . he, too, softly*]: Are you?
That's nice.

[MARTHA's *laugh is heard again.*]

Oh, listen to that.

HONEY: I'm going to die.

GEORGE [*quite by himself now*]: Good . . . good . . . you go right ahead.

[*Very softly, so* MARTHA *could not possibly hear*]

Martha? Martha? I have some . . . terrible news for you.

[*There is a strange half-smile on his lips.*]

It's about our . . . son. He's dead. Can you hear me, Martha? Our boy is dead.

[*He begins to laugh, very softly . . . it is mixed with crying.*]

CURTAIN

ACT THREE

THE EXORCISM

[MARTHA *enters, talking to herself.*]

MARTHA: Hey, hey. . . . Where is everybody . . . ? [*It is evident she is not bothered.*] So? Drop me; pluck me like a goddamn . . . whatever-it-is . . . creeping vine, and throw me over your shoulder like an old shoe . . . George? [*Looks about her.*] George? [*Silence.*] George! What are you doing: Hiding, or something? [*Silence.*] GEORGE! ! [*Silence.*] Oh, fa Chri. . . [*Goes to the bar, makes herself a drink and amuses herself with the following performance.*] Deserted! Abandon-ed! Left out in the cold like an old pussy-cat. HA! Can I get you a drink, Martha? Why, thank you, George; that's very kind of you. No, Martha, no; why I'd do anything for you. Would you, George? Why, I'd do anything for you, too. Would you, Martha? Why, certainly, George. Martha, I've misjudged you. And I've misjudged you, too, George, WHERE IS EVERYBODY!!! Hump the Hostess! [*Laughs greatly at this, falls into a chair; calms down, looks defeated, says, softly*] Fat chance. [*Even softer*] Fat chance. [*Baby-talk now.*] Daddy? Daddy? Martha is abandon-ed. Left to her own vices at. . . [*Peers at a clock*] . . . something o'clock in the old A.M. Daddy White-Mouse; do you really have red eyes? Do you? Let me see. Ohhhhh! You do! You do! Daddy, you have red eyes . . . because you cry all the time, don't you, Daddy. Yes; you do. You cry alllll the time, I'LL GIVE ALL YOU BASTARDS FIVE TO COME OUT FROM WHERE YOU'RE HIDING!! [*Pause*] I cry all the time too, Daddy. I cry alllll the time; but deep inside, so no one can see me. I cry all the time. And Georgie cries all the time, too. We both cry all the time, and then, what we do, we cry, and we take our tears, and we put 'em in the ice box, in the goddamn ice trays [*Begins to laugh*] until they're all frozen [*Laughs even more*] and then . . . we put them . . . in our . . . drinks. [*More laughter, which is something else, too. After sobering silence*] Up the drain, down the spout, dead, gone and forgotten. . . . Up the spout, not down the spout; *up* the spout: THE POKER NIGHT. Up the spout. . . . [*Sadly*] I've got windshield wipers on my eyes, because I married you . . . baby! . . . Martha, you'll be a songwriter yet. [*Jiggles the ice in her glass.*] CLINK! [*Does it again.*] CLINK! [*Giggles, repeats it several times.*] CLINK! . . . CLINK! . . . CLINK! . . . CLINK!

[NICK *enters while* MARTHA *is clinking; he stands in the hall entrance and watches her; finally he comes in.*]

NICK: My God, you've gone crazy too.

MARTHA: Clink?

NICK: I said, you've gone crazy too.

MARTHA [*considers it*]: Probably . . . probably.

NICK: You've all gone crazy: I come downstairs, and what happens. . . .

MARTHA: What happens?

NICK: . . . my wife's gone into the can with a liquor bottle, and she winks at me . . . winks at me! . . .

MARTHA [*sadly*]: She's never wunk at you; what a shame. . . .

NICK: She is lying down on the floor again, the tiles, all curled up, and she starts peeling the label off the liquor bottle, the brandy bottle. . . .

MARTHA: . . . we'll never get the deposit back that way. . . .

NICK: . . . and I ask her what she's doing, and she goes: shhhhhh!, nobody knows I'm here; and I come back in here, and you're sitting there going Clink!, for God's sake. Clink!

MARTHA: CLINK!

NICK: You've all gone crazy.

MARTHA: Yes. Sad but true.

NICK: Where is your husband?

MARTHA: He is vanish-ed. Pouf!

NICK: You're all crazy: nuts.

MARTHA [*affects a brogue*]: Awww, 'tis the refuge we take when the unreality of the world weighs too heavy on our tiny heads. [*Normal voice again*] Relax; sink into it; you're no better than anybody else.

NICK [*wearily*]: I think I am.

MARTHA [*her glass to her mouth*]: You're certainly a flop in some departments.

NICK [*wincing*]: I beg your pardon . . . ?

MARTHA [*unnecessarily loud*]: I said, you're certainly a flop in some . . .

NICK [*he, too, too loud*]: I'm sorry you're disappointed.

MARTHA [*braying*]: I didn't say I was disappointed! Stupid!

NICK: You should try me some time when we haven't been drinking for ten hours, and maybe . . .

MARTHA [*still braying*]: I wasn't talking about your potential; I was talking about your goddamn performance.

NICK [*softly*]: Oh.

MARTHA [*she softer, too*]: Your potential's fine. It's dandy. [*Wiggles her eyebrows*]. Absolutely dandy. I haven't seen such a dandy potential in a long time. Oh, but baby, you sure are a flop.

NICK [*snapping it out*]: Everybody's a flop to you! Your husband's a flop, *I'm* a flop. . . .

MARTHA [*dismissing him*]: You're all flops. I am the Earth Mother, and you're all flops. [*More or less to herself*] I disgust me. I pass my life in crummy, totally pointless infidelities . . . [*Laughs ruefully*] *would*-be infidelities. Hump the Hostess? That's a laugh. A bunch of boozed-up . . . impotent lunk-heads. Martha makes goo-goo eyes, and

the lunk-heads grin, and roll their beautiful, beautiful eyes
back, and grin some more, and Martha licks her chops, and
the lunk-heads slap over to the bar to pick up a little
courage, *and* they pick up a little courage, and they bounce
back over to old Martha, who does a little dance for them,
which heats them all up . . . mentally . . . and so they slap
over to the bar again, and pick up a little more courage, and
their wives and sweethearts stick their noses up in the air
. . . right through the ceiling, sometimes . . . which sends the
lunk-heads back to the soda fountain again where they fuel
up some more, while Martha-poo sits there with her dress
up over her head . . . suffocating – you don't know how
stuffy it is with your dress up over your head – suffocating!
waiting for the lunk-heads; so, *finally* they get their courage
up . . . but that's all, baby! Oh my, there is sometimes some
very nice potential, but, oh my! My, my, my. [*Brightly*] But
that's how it is in a civilized society. [*To herself again*] All
the gorgeous lunk-heads. Poor babies. [*To* NICK, *now*;
earnestly] There is only one man in my life who has ever . . .
made me happy. Do you know that? One!

NICK: The . . . the what-do-you-call-it? . . . uh . . . the lawn
mower, or something?

MARTHA: No; I'd forgotten him. But when I think about him
and me it's almost like being a voyeur. Hunh. No; I didn't
mean him; I meant George, of course. [*No response from*
NICK.] Uh . . . George; my husband.

NICK [*disbelieving*]: You're kidding.

MARTHA: Am I?

NICK: You must be. Him?

MARTHA: Him.

NICK [*as if in on a joke*]: Sure; sure.

MARTHA: You don't believe it.

NICK [*mocking*]: Why, of course I do.

MARTHA: You always deal in appearances?

NICK [*derisively*]: Oh, for God's sake. . . .

MARTHA: . . . George who is out somewhere there in the dark. . . . George who is good to me, and whom I revile; who understands me, and whom I push off; who can make me laugh, and I choke it back in my throat; who can hold me, at night, so that it's warm, and whom I will bite so there's blood; who keeps learning the games we play as quickly as I can change the rules; who can make me happy and I do not wish to be happy, and yes I do wish to be happy. George and Martha: sad, sad, sad.

NICK [*echoing, still not believing*]: Sad.

MARTHA: . . . whom I will not forgive for having come to rest; for having seen me and having said: yes; this will do; who has made the hideous, the hurting, the insulting mistake of loving me and must be punished for it. George and Martha: sad, sad, sad.

NICK [*puzzled*]: Sad.

MARTHA: . . . who tolerates, which is intolerable; who is kind, which is cruel; who understands, which is beyond comprehension. . . .

NICK: George and Martha: sad, sad, sad.

MARTHA: Some day . . . hah! some *night* . . . some stupid, liquor-ridden night. . . I will go too far . . . and I'll either break the man's back . . . or push him off for good . . . which is what I deserve.

NICK: I don't think he's got a vertebra intact.

MARTHA [*laughing at him*]: You don't, huh? You don't think so. Oh, little boy, you got yourself hunched over that microphone of yours. . . .

NICK: Microscope. . . .

MARTHA: . . . yes . . . and you don't see anything, do you? You see everything but the goddamn mind; you see all the little specs and crap, but you don't see what goes on, do you?

NICK: I know when a man's had his back broken; I can see that.

MARTHA: Can you!

NICK: You're damn right.

MARTHA: Oh . . . you know so little. And you're going to take over the world, hunh?

NICK: All right, now. . . .

MARTHA: You think a man's got his back broken 'cause he makes like a clown and walks bent, hunh? Is that *really* all you know?

NICK: I said, all *right*!

MARTHA: Ohhhh! The stallion's mad, hunh. The gelding's all upset. Ha, ha, ha, HA!

NICK [*softly; wounded*]: You . . . you swing wild, don't you.

MARTHA [*triumphant*]: HAH!

NICK: Just. . . anywhere.

MARTHA: HAH! I'm a gattling gun. Hahahahahahahahaha!

NICK [*in wonder*]: Aimless . . . butchery. Pointless.

MARTHA: Aw! You poor little bastard.

NICK: Hit out at everything.

[*The door chimes chime.*]

MARTHA: Go answer the door.

NICK [*amazed*]: What did you say?

MARTHA: I said, go answer the door. What are you, deaf?

NICK [*trying to get it straight*]: You . . . want me . . . to go answer the door?

MARTHA: That's right, lunk-head; answer the door. There must be something you can do well; or, are you too drunk to do that, too? Can't you get the latch up, either?

NICK: Look, there's no need . . .

[*Door chimes again.*]

MARTHA [*shouting*]: Answer it! [*Softer*] You can be houseboy around here for a while. You can start off being houseboy right now.

NICK: Look, lady, I'm no flunky to you.

MARTHA [*cheerfully*]: Sure you are! You're ambitious, aren't you, boy? You didn't chase me around the kitchen and up the goddamn stairs out of mad, driven passion, did you now? You were thinking a little bit about your career, weren't you? Well, you can just houseboy your way up the ladder for a while.

NICK: There's no limit to you, is there?

[*Door chimes again.*]

MARTHA [*calmly, surely*]: No, baby; none. Go answer the door, [NICK *hesitates.*] Look, boy; once you stick your nose in it, you're not going to pull out just whenever you feel like it. You're in for a while. Now, git!

NICK: Aimless . . . wanton . . . pointless. . . .

MARTHA: Now, now, now; just do what you're told; show old Martha there's something you *can* do. Hunh? Atta boy.

NICK [*considers, gives in, moves towards the door. Chimes again*]: I'm coming, for Christ's sake!

MARTHA [*claps her hands*]: Ha HA! Wonderful; marvellous. [*Sings*] 'Just a gigolo, everywhere I go, people always say . . .'

NICK: STOP THAT!

MARTHA [*giggles*]: Sorry, baby; go on now; open the little door.

NICK [*with great rue*]: Christ.

[*He flings open the door, and a hand thrusts into the opening a great bunch of snapdragons; they stay there for a moment.* NICK *strains his eyes to see who is behind them.*]

MARTHA: Oh, how lovely!

GEORGE [*appearing in the doorway, the snapdragons covering his face; speaks in a hideously cracked falsetto*]: Flores; flores para los muertos. Flores.

MARTHA: Ha, ha, ha, HA!

GEORGE: [*a step into the room; lowers the flowers; sees* NICK; *his face becomes gleeful; he opens his arms*]: Sonny! You've come home for your birthday! At last!

NICK [*backing off*]: Stay away from me.

MARTHA: Ha, ha, ha, HA! That's the houseboy, for God's sake.

GEORGE: Really? That's not our own little sonny-Jim? Our own little all-American something-or-other?

MARTHA [*giggling*]: Well, I certainly hope not; he's been acting awful funny, if he is.

GEORGE [*almost manic*]: Ohhhh! I'll bet! Chippie-chippie-chippie, hunh? [*Affecting embarrassment*] I . . . I brungya dese flowers, Mart'a, 'cause I . . . wull, 'cause you'se . . . awwwwww hell. Gee.

MARTHA: Pansies! Rosemary! Violence! My wedding bouquet!

NICK [*starting to move away*]: Well, if you two kids don't mind, I think I'll just . . .

MARTHA: Ach! You just stay where you are. Make my hubby a drink.

NICK: I don't think I will.

GEORGE: No, Martha, no; that would be too much; he's your houseboy, baby, not mine.

NICK: I'm nobody's houseboy. . . .

GEORGE *and* MARTHA: . . . Now! [*Sing*] I'm nobody's houseboy now. . . . [*Both laugh.*]

NICK: Vicious . . .

GEORGE [*finishing it for him*]: . . . children. Hunh? That right? Vicious children, with their oh-so-sad games, hopscotching their way through life, etcetera, etcetera. Is that it?

NICK: Something like it.

GEORGE: Screw, baby.

MARTHA: Him can't. Him too fulla booze.

GEORGE: Weally? [*Handing the snapdragons to* NICK] Here; dump these in some gin. [NICK *takes them, looks at them, drops them on the floor at his feet.*]

MARTHA [*sham dismay*]: Awwwwwww.

GEORGE: What a terrible thing to do . . . to Martha's snapdragons.

MARTHA: Is that what they are?

GEORGE: Yup. And here I went out into the moonlight to pick 'em for Martha tonight, and for our sonny-boy tomorrow, for his birfday.

MARTHA [*passing on information*]: There is no moon now. I saw it go down from the bedroom.

GEORGE [*feigned glee*]: From the bedroom! [*Normal tone*] Well, there was a moon.

MARTHA [*too patient; laughing a little*]: There couldn't have been a moon.

GEORGE: Well, there was. There is.

MARTHA: There is no moon; the moon went down.

GEORGE: There is a moon; the moon is up.

MARTHA [*straining to keep civil*]: I'm afraid you're mistaken.

GEORGE [*too cheerful*]: No; no.

MARTHA [*between her teeth*]: There is no goddamn moon.

GEORGE: My dear Martha . . . I did not pick snapdragons in the stony dark. I did not go stumbling around Daddy's greenhouse in the pitch.

MARTHA: Yes . . . you did. You would.

GEORGE: Martha, I do not pick flowers in the blink. I have never robbed a hothouse without there is a light from heaven.

MARTHA [*with finality*]: There is no moon; the moon went down.

GEORGE [*with great logic*]: That may very well be, Chastity; the moon may very well have gone down . . . but it came back up.

MARTHA: The moon does *not* come back up; when the moon has gone down it stays down.

GEORGE [*getting a little ugly*]: You don't know anything. If the moon went down, then it came back up.

MARTHA: BULL!

GEORGE: Ignorance! Such . . . ignorance.

MARTHA: Watch who you're calling ignorant!

GEORGE: Once . . . once, when I was sailing past Majorca,

drinking on deck with a correspondent who was talking about Roosevelt, the moon went down, thought about it for a little . . . considered it, you know what I mean? . . . and then, POP, came up again. Just like that.

MARTHA: That is not true! That is such a lie!

GEORGE: You must not call everything a lie, Martha. [*To* NICK] Must she?

NICK: Hell, I don't know when you people are lying, or what.

MARTHA: You're damned right!

GEORGE: You're not supposed to.

MARTHA: Right!

GEORGE: At any rate, I was sailing past Majorca. . . .

MARTHA: You never sailed past Majorca. . . .

GEORGE: Martha. . . .

MARTHA: You were never in the goddamn Mediterranean at all . . . ever. . . .

GEORGE: I certainly was! My mommy and daddy took me there as a college graduation present.

MARTHA: Nuts!

NICK: Was this after you killed them?

[GEORGE *and* MARTHA *swing around and look at him; there is a brief, ugly pause.*]

GEORGE [*defiantly*]: Maybe.

MARTHA: Yeah; maybe not, too.

NICK: Jesus!

[GEORGE *swoops down, picks up the bunch of snapdragons, shakes them like a feather duster in* NICK'S *face, and moves away a little.*]

GEORGE: HAH!

NICK: Damn you.

GEORGE [*to* NICK]: Truth and illusion. Who knows the difference, eh, toots? Eh?

MARTHA: You were never in the Mediterranean . . . truth or illusion . . . either way.

GEORGE: If I wasn't in the Mediterranean, how did I get to the Aegean? Hunh?

MARTHA: OVERLAND!

NICK: Yeah!

GEORGE: Don't you side with her, houseboy.

NICK: I am not a houseboy.

GEORGE: Look! I know the game! You don't make it in the sack, you're a houseboy.

NICK: I AM NOT A HOUSEBOY!

GEORGE: No? Well then, you must have made it in the sack. Yes? [*He is breathing a little heavy; behaving a little manic*] Yes? Someone's lying around here; somebody isn't playing the game straight. Yes? Come on; come on; who's lying? Martha? Come on!

NICK [*after a pause; to* MARTHA, *quietly with intense pleading*]: Tell him I'm not a houseboy.

MARTHA [*after a pause, quietly, lowering her head*]: No; you're not a houseboy.

GEORGE [*with great, sad relief*]: So be it.

MARTHA [*pleading*]: Truth and illusion, George; you don't know the difference.

GEORGE: No; but we must carry on as though we did.

MARTHA: Amen.

GEORGE [*flourishing the flowers*]: SNAP WENT THE DRAGONS!! [NICK *and* MARTHA *laugh weakly.*] Hunh? Here we go round the mulberry bush, Hunh?

NICK [*tenderly, to* MARTHA]: Thank you.

MARTHA: Skip it.

GEORGE [*loud*]: I said, here we go round the mulberry bush!

MARTHA [*impatiently*]: Yeah, yeah; we know; snap go the dragons.

GEORGE [*taking a snapdragon, throwing it, spear-like, stem-first at* MARTHA]: SNAP!

MARTHA: Don't, George.

GEORGE [*throws another*]: SNAP!

NICK: Don't do that.

GEORGE: Shut up, stud.

NICK: I'm not a stud!

GEORGE [*throws one at* NICK]: SNAP! Then you're a house-boy. Which is it? Which are you? Hunh? Make up your mind. Either way . . . [*Throws another at him.*] SNAP! . . . *you disgust me.*

MARTHA: Does it matter to you, George!?

GEORGE [*throws one at her*]: SNAP! No, actually, it doesn't. Either way . . . I've had it.

MARTHA: Stop throwing those goddamn things at me!

GEORGE: Either way. [*Throws another at her*] SNAP!

NICK [*to* MARTHA]: Do you want me to . . . do something to him?

MARTHA: You leave him alone!

GEORGE: If you're a houseboy, baby, you can pick up after me; if you're a stud, you can go protect your plough. Either way. Either way. . . . Everything.

NICK: Oh for God's . . .

MARTHA [*a little afraid*]: Truth or illusion, George. Doesn't it matter to you . . . at all?

GEORGE [*without throwing anything*]: SNAP! [*Silence.*] You got your answer, baby?

MARTHA [*sadly*]: Got it.

GEORGE: You just gird your blue-veined loins, girl. [*Sees* NICK *moving towards the hall.*] Now; we got one more game to play. And it's called bringing up baby.

NICK [*more-or-less under his breath*]: Oh, for Lord's sake. . . .

MARTHA: George. . . .

GEORGE: I don't want any fuss. [*To* NICK] You don't want any scandal around here, do you, big boy? You don't want to wreck things, do you? Hunh? You want to keep to your time-table, don't you? Then sit! [NICK *sits. To* MARTHA] And you, pretty Miss, you like fun and games, don't you? You're a sport from way back, aren't you?

MARTHA [*quietly, giving in*]: All right, George, all right.

GEORGE [*seeing them both cowed; purrs*]: Gooooooooood; gooooood. [*Looks about him.*] But, we're not all here. [*Snaps his fingers a couple of times at* NICK.] You; you . . . uh . . . you; your little wifelet isn't here.

NICK: Look; she's had a rough night, now; she's in the can, and she's . . .

GEORGE: Well, we can't play without everyone here. Now that's a fact. We gotta have your little wife. [*Hog-calls towards the hall*] SOOOWWWIIIEEE!! SOOOWWWIIIEEE!!

NICK [*as* MARTHA *giggles nervously*]: Cut that!

GEORGE [*swinging around, facing him*]: Then get your butt out of that chair and bring the little dip back in here. [*As* NICK *does not move*] Now be a good puppy. Fetch, good puppy, go fetch.

[NICK *rises, opens his mouth to say something, thinks better of it, exits.*]

One more game.

MARTHA [*after* NICK *goes*]: I don't like what's going to happen.

GEORGE [*surprisingly tender*]: Do you know what it is?

MARTHA [*pathetic*]: No. But I don't like it.

GEORGE: Maybe you will, Martha.

MARTHA: No.

GEORGE: Oh, it's a real fun game, Martha.

MARTHA [*pleading*]: No more games.

GEORGE [*quietly triumphant*]: One more, Martha. One more game, and then beddie-bye. Everybody pack up his tools and baggage and stuff and go home. And you and me, well, we gonna climb them well-worn stairs.

MARTHA [*almost in tears*]: No, George; no.

GEORGE [*soothing*]: Yes, baby.

MARTHA: No, George; please?

GEORGE: It'll all be done with before you know it.

MARTHA: No, George.

GEORGE: No climb stairs with Georgie?

MARTHA [*a sleepy child*]: No more games . . . please. It's games I don't want. No more games.

GEORGE: Aw, sure you do, Martha . . . original game-girl and all, 'course you do.

MARTHA: Ugly games . . . ugly. And now this new one?

GEORGE [*stroking her hair*]: You'll love it, baby.

MARTHA: No George.

GEORGE: You'll have a ball.

MARTHA [*tenderly; moves to touch him*]: Please, George, no more games; I . . .

GEORGE [*slapping her moving hand with vehemence*]: Don't you touch me! You keep your paws clean for the under-graduates!

MARTHA [*a cry of alarm, but faint.*]

GEORGE [*grabbing her hair, pulling her head back*]: Now, you listen to me, Martha; you have had quite an evening . . . quite a night for yourself, and you can't just cut it off when-ever you've got enough blood in your mouth. We are going on, and I'm going to have at you, and it's going to make your performance tonight look like an Easter pageant. Now I want you to get yourself a little alert. [*Slaps her lightly with his free hand.*] I want a little life in you, baby. [*Again.*]

MARTHA [*struggling*]: Stop it!

GEORGE [*again*]: Pull yourself together! [*Again.*] I want you on your feet and slugging, sweetheart, because I'm going to knock you around, and I want you up for it. [*Again; he pulls away, releases her; she rises.*]

MARTHA: All right, George. What do you want, George?

GEORGE: An equal battle, baby; that's all.

MARTHA: You'll get it!

GEORGE: I want you mad.

MARTHA: I'M MAD!!

GEORGE: Get madder!

MARTHA: DON'T WORRY ABOUT IT!

GEORGE: Good for you, girl; now, we're going to play this
   one to the death.

MARTHA: Yours!

GEORGE: You'd be surprised. Now, here come the tots; you
   be ready for this.

MARTHA [*she paces, actually looks a bit like a fighter*]: I'm
   ready for you.

   [NICK *and* HONEY *re-enter;* NICK *supporting* HONEY,
   who still retains her brandy bottle and glass.]

NICK [*unhappily*]: Here we are.

HONEY [*cheerfully*]: Hip, hop. Hip, hop.

NICK: You a bunny, Honey? [*She laughs greatly, sits.*]

HONEY: I'm a bunny, Honey.

GEORGE [*to* HONEY]: Well, now; how's the bunny?

HONEY: Bunny funny! [*She laughs again.*]

NICK [*under his breath*]: Jesus.

GEORGE: Bunny funny? Good for bunny!

MARTHA: Come on, George!

GEORGE [*to* MARTHA]: Honey funny bunny! [HONEY
   screams with laughter.]

NICK: Jesus God. . . .

GEORGE [*slaps his hands together, once*]: All right! Here we
   go! Last game! All sit. [NICK *sits.*] Sit down, Martha. This
   is a civilized game.

MARTHA [*cocks her fist, doesn't swing. Sits*]: Just get on with
   it.

HONEY [*to* GEORGE]: I've decided I don't remember anything. [*To* NICK] Hello, dear.

GEORGE: Hunh? What?

MARTHA: It's almost dawn, for God's sake. . . .

HONEY [*ibid.*]: I don't remember anything, and you don't
   remember anything, either. Hello, dear.

GEORGE: You what?

HONEY [*ibid. An edge creeping into her voice*]: You heard
   me, nothing. Hello, dear.

GEORGE [*to* HONEY, *referring* to NICK]: You do know that's your husband, there, don't you?

HONEY [*with great dignity*]: Well, I certainly know *that*.

GEORGE [*close to* HONEY's *ear*]: It's just some things you can't remember . . . hunh?

HONEY [*a great laugh to cover; then quietly, intensely to* GEORGE]: *Don't* remember; not *can't*. [*At* NICK, *cheerfully*] Hello, dear.

GEORGE [*to* NICK]: Well, speak to your little wifelet, your little bunny, for God's sake.

NICK [*softly, embarrassed*]: Hello, Honey.

GEORGE: Awww, that was nice. I think we've been having a . . . a real good evening . . . all things considered. . . . We've sat around, and got to know each other, and had fun and games . . . curl-up-on-the-floor, for example. . . .

HONEY: . . . the tiles. . . .

GEORGE: . . . the tiles. . . . Snap the Dragon.

HONEY: . . . peel the label. . . .

GEORGE: . . . peel the . . . what?

MARTHA: Label. Peel the label.

HONEY [*apologetically, holding up her brandy bottle*]: I peel labels.

GEORGE: We all peel labels, sweetie; and when you get through the skin, all three layers, through the muscle, slosh aside the organs [*An aside to* NICK] them which is still sloshable – [*Back* to HONEY] and get down to bone . . . you know what you do then?

HONEY [*terribly interested*]: No!

GEORGE: When you get down to bone, you haven't got all the way, yet. There's something inside the bone . . . the marrow . . . and that's what you gotta get at. [*A strange smile at* MARTHA.]

HONEY: Oh! I see.

GEORGE: The marrow. But bones are pretty resilient, especially in the young. Now, take our son . . .

HONEY [*strangely*]: Who?

GEORGE: Our son . . . Martha's and my little joy!

NICK [*moving towards the bar*]: Do you mind if I . . . ?

GEORGE: No, no; you go right ahead.

MARTHA: George. . . .

GEORGE [*too kindly*]: Yes, Martha?

MARTHA: Just what are you doing?

GEORGE: Why love, I was talking about our son.

MARTHA: Don't.

GEORGE: Isn't Martha something? Here we are, on the eve of our boy's home-coming, the eve of his twenty-first birfday, the eve of his majority . . . and Martha says don't talk about him.

MARTHA: Just . . . don't.

GEORGE: But I want to, Martha! It's very important we talk about him. Now bunny and the . . . well, whichever he is . . . here don't know much about junior, and I think they should.

MARTHA: Just . . . don't.

GEORGE [*snapping his fingers at* NICK]: You. Hey, you! You want to play bringing up baby, don't you!

NICK [*hardly civil*]: Were you snapping at me?

GEORGE: That's right. [*Instructing him*] *You* want to hear about our bouncey boy.

NICK [*pause; then, shortly*]: Yeah; sure.

GEORGE [*to* HONEY]: And you, my dear? You want to hear about him, too, don't you.

HONEY [*pretending not to understand*]: Whom?

GEORGE: Martha's and my son.

HONEY [*nervously*]: Oh, you have a child?

[MARTHA *and* NICK *laugh uncomfortably.*]

GEORGE: Oh, indeed; do we ever! Do you want to talk about him, Martha, or shall I? Hunh?

MARTHA [*a smile that is a sneer*]: Don't, George.

GEORGE: All rightie. Well, now; let's see. He's a nice kid,

really, in spite of his home life; I mean, most kids'd grow up neurotic, what with Martha here carrying on the way she does: sleeping till four in the P.M., climbing all over the poor bastard, trying to break the bathroom door down to wash him in the tub when he's sixteen, dragging strangers into the house at all hours. . . .

MARTHA [*rising*]: O.K. YOU!

GEORGE [*mock concern*]: Martha!

MARTHA: That's enough!

GEORGE: Well, do you want to take over?

HONEY [*to* NICK]: Why would anybody want to wash somebody who's sixteen years old?

NICK [*slamming his drink down*]: Oh, for Christ's sake, Honey!

HONEY [*stage whisper*]: Well, why?

GEORGE: Because it's her baby-poo.

MARTHA: ALL RIGHT!!

　　[*By rote; a kind of almost-tearful recitation*]
　　Our son. You want our son? You'll have it.

GEORGE: You want a drink, Martha?

MARTHA [*pathetically*]: Yes.

NICK [*to* MARTHA *kindly*]: We don't have to hear about it . . . if you don't want to.

GEORGE: Who says so? You in a position to set the rules around here?

NICK [*pause; tight-lipped*]: No.

GEORGE: Good boy; you'll go far. All right, Martha; your recitation, please.

MARTHA [*from far away*]: What, George?

GEORGE [*prompting*]: 'Our son . . .'

MARTHA: All right. Our son. Our son was born in a September night, a night not unlike tonight, though tomorrow, and twenty . . . one . . . years ago.

GEORGE [*beginning of quiet asides*]: You see? I told you.

MARTHA: It was an easy birth. . . .

GEORGE: Oh, Martha; no. You laboured . . . how you laboured.

MARTHA: It was an easy birth . . . once it had been . . . accepted, relaxed into.

GEORGE: Ah . . . yes. Better.

MARTHA: It was an easy birth, once it had been accepted, and I was young.

GEORGE: And I was younger. . . . [*Laughs quietly to himself.*]

MARTHA: And I was young, and he was a healthy child, a red, bawling child, with slippery firm limbs . . .

GEORGE: . . . Martha thinks she saw him at delivery. . . .

MARTHA: . . . with slippery, firm limbs, and a full head of black, fine, fine hair which, oh, later, later, became blond as the sun, our son.

GEORGE: He was a healthy child.

MARTHA: And I had wanted a child . . . oh, I had wanted a child.

GEORGE [*prodding her*]: A son? A daughter?

MARTHA: A child! [*Quieter*] A child. And I had my child.

GEORGE: Our child.

MARTHA [*with great sadness*]: *Our* child. And we raised him . . . [*Laughs, briefly, bitterly.*] . . . yes, we did; we raised him . . .

GEORGE: With teddy bears and an antique bassinet from Austria . . . and *no nurse.*

MARTHA: . . . with teddy bears and transparent floating goldfish, and a pale blue bed with cane at the headboard when he was older, cane which he wore through . . . finally . . . with his little hands . . . in his . . . sleep. . . .

GEORGE: . . . nightmares. . . .

MARTHA: . . . *sleep.* . . . He was a restless child. . . .

GEORGE: . . . [*Soft chuckle, head-shaking of disbelief.*] . . . Oh Lord. . . .

MARTHA: . . . sleep . . . and a croup tent. . . a pale green croup tent, and the shining kettle hissing in the one light of the

room that time he was sick . . . those four days . . . and
animal crackers, and the bow and arrow he kept under his
bed. . . .

GEORGE: . . . the arrows with rubber cups at their tip . . .

MARTHA: . . . at their tip, which he kept beneath his bed . . . .

GEORGE: Why? Why, Martha?

MARTHA: . . . for fear . . . for fear of . . .

GEORGE: For fear. Just that: for fear.

MARTHA [*vaguely waving him off; going on*]: . . . and . . . and
sandwiches on Sunday night, and Saturdays . . . [*Pleased
recollection*] . . . and Saturdays the banana boat, the whole
peeled banana, scooped out on top, with green grapes for
the crew, a double line of green grapes, and along the sides,
stuck to the boat with toothpicks, orange slices. . . . SHIELDS.

GEORGE: And for the oar?

MARTHA [*uncertainly*]: A . . . carrot?

GEORGE: Or a swizzle stick, whatever was easier.

MARTHA: No. A carrot. And his eyes were green . . . green
with . . . if you peered so deep into them . . . so deep . . .
bronze . . . bronze parentheses around the irises . . . such
green eyes!

GEORGE: . . . blue, green, brown. . . .

MARTHA: . . . and he loved the sun! . . . He was tan before
and after everyone . . . and in the sun his hair . . . became .
. . fleece.

GEORGE [*echoing her*]: . . . fleece. . . .

MARTHA: . . . beautiful, beautiful boy.

GEORGE: Absolve, Domine, animas omnium fidelium de-
functorum ab omni vinculo delictorum.

MARTHA: . . . and school . . . and summer camp . . . and
sledding . . . and swimming. . . .

GEORGE: Et gratia tua illis succurrente, mereantur evadere
judicium ultionis.

MARTHA [*laughing, to herself*]: . . . and how he broke his arm
. . . how funny it was . . . oh, no, it hurt him! . . . but, oh,

it was funny . . . in a field, his very first cow, the first he'd ever seen . . . and he went into the field, to the cow, where the cow was grazing, head down, busy . . . and he moo'd at it! [*Laughs, ibid.*] He moo'd at it. . . and the beast, oh, surprised, swung its head up and moo'd at him, all three years of him, and he ran, startled, and he stumbled . . . fell . . . and broke his poor arm. [*Laughs, ibid.*] Poor lamb.

GEORGE: Et lucis aeternae beatitudine perfrui.

MARTHA: George cried! Helpless . . . George . . . cried. I carried the poor lamb. George snuffling beside me, I carried the child, having fashioned a sling . . . and across the great fields.

GEORGE: In Paradisum deducant te Angeli.

MARTHA: And as he grew . . . and as he grew . . . oh! so wise! . . . he walked evenly between us . . . [*She spreads her hands.*] . . . a hand out to each of us for what we could offer by way of support, affection, teaching, even love . . . and these hands, still, to hold us off a bit, for mutual protection, to protect us all from George's . . . weakness . . . and my . . . necessary greater strength . . . to protect himself . . . and *us.*

GEORGE: In memoria aeterna erit justus: ab auditione mala non timebit.

MARTHA: So wise; so wise.

NICK [*to* GEORGE]: What is this? What are you doing?

GEORGE: Shhhhh.

HONEY: Shhhhh.

NICK [*shrugging*]: O.K.

MARTHA: So beautiful; so wise.

GEORGE [*laughs quietly*]: All truth being relative.

MARTHA: It was true! Beautiful; wise; perfect.

GEORGE: There's a real mother talking.

HONEY [*suddenly; almost tearfully*]: I want a child.

NICK: Honey. . . .

HONEY [*more forcefully*]: I want a child!

GEORGE: On principle?

HONEY [*in tears*]: I want a child. I want a baby.

MARTHA [*waiting out the interruption, not really paying it any mind*]: Of course, this state, this perfection . . . couldn't last. Not with George . . . not with George around.

GEORGE [*to the others*]: There; you see? I knew she'd shift.

HONEY: Be still!

GEORGE [*mock awe*]: Sorry . . . mother.

NICK: Can't you be still?

GEORGE [*making a sign at* NICK]: Dominus vobiscum.

MARTHA: Not with George around. A drowning man takes down those nearest. George tried, but, oh, God, how I fought him. God, how I fought him.

GEORGE [*a satisfied laugh*]: Ahhhhhhh.

MARTHA: Lesser states can't stand those above them. Weakness, imperfection cries out against strength, goodness and innocence. And George tried.

GEORGE: How did I try, Martha? How did I try?

MARTHA: How did you . . . what? . . . No! No . . . he grew . . . our son grew . . . up; he is grown up; he is away at school, college. He is fine, everything is fine.

GEORGE [*mocking*]: Oh, come on, Martha!

MARTHA No. That's all.

GEORGE: Just a minute! You can't cut a story off like that, sweetheart. You started to say something . . . now you say it!

MARTHA: No!

GEORGE: Well, I will.

MARTHA: No!

GEORGE: You see, Martha, here, stops just when the going gets good . . . just when things start getting a little rough. Now, Martha, here, is a misunderstood little girl; she really is. Not only does she have a husband who is a bog . . . a younger-than-she-is bog albeit . . . not only does she have a husband who is a bog, she has as well a tiny problem with spirituous liquors – like she can't get enough. . . .

MARTHA [*without energy*]: No more, George.

GEORGE: . . . and on top of all that, poor weighed-down girl, PLUS a father who really doesn't give a damn whether she lives or dies, who couldn't care less *what* happens to his only daughter . . . on top of all that she has a *son*. She has a son who fought her every inch of the way, who didn't want to be turned into a weapon against his father, who didn't want to be used as a goddamn club whenever Martha didn't get things like she wanted them!

MARTHA [*rising to it*]: Lies! Lies!!

GEORGE: Lies? All right. A son who would *not* disown his father, who came to him for advice, for information, for love that wasn't mixed with sickness – and you know what I mean, Martha! – who could not tolerate the slashing, braying residue that called itself his MOTHER. MOTHER? HAH!!

MARTHA [*cold*]: All right, you. A son who was so ashamed of his father he asked me once if it – possibly – wasn't true, as he had heard, from some cruel boys, maybe, that he was not our child; who could not tolerate the shabby failure his father had become. . . .

GEORGE: Lies!

MARTHA: Lies? Who would not bring his girl friends to the house . . .

GEORGE: . . . in shame of his mother. . . .

MARTHA: . . . of his father! Who writes letters only to me!

GEORGE: Oh, so you think! To me! At my office!

MARTHA: Liar!

GEORGE: I have a stack of them!

MARTHA: YOU HAVE NO LETTERS!

GEORGE: And you have?

MARTHA: He has no letters. A son . . . a son who spends his summers away . . . away from his family . . . ON ANY PRETEXT . . . because he can't stand the shadow of a man flickering around the edges of a house. . . .

GEORGE: . . . who spends his summers away . . . and he does!
. . . who spends his summers away because there isn't room
for him in a house full of empty bottles, lies, strange men,
and a harridan who . . .

MARTHA: Liar!!

GEORGE: Liar?

MARTHA: . . . A son who I have raised as best I can against
. . . vicious odds, against the corruption of weakness and
petty revenges. . . .

GEORGE: . . . A son who is, deep in his gut, sorry to have been
born. . . .

[*Both together.*]

MARTHA: I have tried, oh God I have tried; the one thing . . . the one thing I've tried to carry pure and unscathed through the sewer of this marriage; through the sick nights, and the pathetic, stupid days, through the laughter . . . *God*, the laughter, through one failure after another, one failure compounding another failure, each attempt more sickening, more numbing than the one before; the one thing, the one *person* I have tried to protect, to raise above the mire of this vile, crushing marriage; the one light in all this hopeless . . . *dark*ness our SON.

GEORGE: Libera me, Domine, de morte aeterna, in die illa tremenda: Quando caeli movendi sunt et terra: Dum veneris judicare saeculum per ignem. Tremes factus sum ego, et timeo, dum discussio venerit, atque venture ira. Quando caeli movendi sunt et terra. Dies illa, dies irae, calemitatis et miseriae; dies magna et amara valde. Dum veneris judicare saeculum per ignem. Requiem aeternam dona eis, Domine: et lux perpetua luceat eis. Libera me Domine de morte aeterna in die illa tremenda: quando caeli movendi sunt et terra; Dum veneris judicare saeculum per ignem.

[*End together.*]

HONEY [*her hands to her ears*]: STOP IT!! STOP IT!!

GEORGE [*with a hand sign*]: Kyrie, eleison. Christe, eleison. Kyrie, eleison.

HONEY: JUST STOP IT!!

GEORGE: Why, baby? Don't you like it?

HONEY [*quite hysterical*]: You . . . can't . . . do . . . this!

GEORGE [*triumphant*]: Who says!

HONEY: I! Say!

GEORGE: Tell us why, baby.

HONEY: No!

NICK: Is this game over?

HONEY: Yes! Yes, it is.

GEORGE: Ho-ho! Not by a long shot. [*To* MARTHA] We got a little surprise for you, baby. It's about sunny-Jim.

MARTHA: No more, George.

GEORGE: YES!

NICK: Leave her be!

GEORGE: I'M RUNNING THIS SHOW! [*To* MARTHA] Sweetheart, I'm afraid I've got some bad news for you . . . for us, of course. Some rather sad news.

[HONEY *begins weeping, head in hands.*]

MARTHA [*afraid, suspicious*]: What is this?

GEORGE [*oh, so patiently*]: Well, Martha, while you were out of the room, while the . . . two of you were out of the room . . . I mean, I don't know where, hell, you both must have been somewhere [*Little laugh*]. . . . While you were out of the room, for a while . . . well, Missey and I were sittin' here havin' a little talk, you know: a chaw and a talk . . . and the doorbell rang. . . .

HONEY [*head still in hands*]: Chimed.

GEORGE: Chimed . . . and . . . well, it's hard to tell you, Martha. . . .

MARTHA [*a strange throaty voice*]: Tell me.

HONEY: Please . . . don't.

MARTHA: Tell me.

GEORGE: . . . and . . . what it was . . . it was good old Western

Union, some little boy about seventy.

MARTHA [*involved*]: Crazy Billy?

GEORGE: Yes, Martha, that's right . . . crazy Billy . . . and he had a telegram, and it was for us, and I have to tell you about it.

MARTHA [*as if from a distance*]: Why didn't they phone it? Why did they bring it; why didn't they telephone it?

GEORGE: Some telegrams you have to deliver, Martha; some telegrams you can't phone.

MARTHA [*rising*]: What do you mean?

GEORGE: Martha. . . . I can hardly bring myself to say it . . .

HONEY: Don't.

GEORGE [*to* HONEY]: Do you want to do it?

HONEY [*as if defending herself against an attack of bees*]: No no no no no.

GEORGE [*sighing heavily*]: All right. Well, Martha . . . I'm afraid our boy isn't coming home for his birthday.

MARTHA: Of course he is.

GEORGE: No, Martha.

MARTHA: Of course he is. I say he is!

GEORGE: He . . . can't.

MARTHA: He is! I say so!

GEORGE: Martha . . . [*Long pause*] . . . our son is . . . dead.
    [*Silence.*]
    He was . . . killed . . . late in the afternoon . . .
    [*Silence.*]
    [*A tiny chuckle*] on a country road, with his learner's permit in his pocket, he swerved, to avoid a porcupine, and drove straight into a . . .

MARTHA [*rigid fury*]: YOU . . . CAN'T . . . DO . . . THAT!

GEORGE: . . . large tree.

MARTHA: YOU CANNOT DO THAT!

NICK [*softly*]: Oh my God. [HONEY *is weeping louder.*]

GEORGE [*quietly, dispassionately*]: I thought you should know.

NICK: Oh my God; no.

MARTHA [*quivering with rage and loss*]: NO! NO! YOU CANNOT DO THAT! YOU CAN'T DECIDE THAT FOR YOURSELF! I WILL NOT LET YOU DO THAT!

GEORGE: We'll have to leave around noon, I suppose . . .

MARTHA: I WILL NOT LET YOU DECIDE THESE THINGS!

GEORGE: . . . because there are matters of identification, naturally, and arrangements to be made. . . .

MARTHA [*leaping at* GEORGE, *but ineffectual*]: YOU CAN'T DO THIS!

[NICK *rises, grabs hold of* MARTHA, *pins her arms behind her back.*]

I WON'T LET YOU DO THIS, GET YOUR HANDS OFF ME!

GEORGE [*as* NICK *holds on; right in* MARTHA'*s face*]: You don't seem to understand, Martha; I haven't done anything. Now, pull yourself together. Our son is DEAD! Can you get that into your head?

MARTHA: YOU CAN'T DECIDE THESE THINGS.

NICK: Lady, please.

MARTHA: LET ME GO!

GEORGE: Now listen, Martha; listen carefully. We got a telegram; there was a car accident, and he's dead, POUF! Just like that! Now, how do you like it?

MARTHA [*a howl which weakens into a moan*]: NOOOO-OOoooooo.

GEORGE [*to* NICK]: Let her go. [MARTHA *slumps to the floor in a sitting position.*] She'll be all right now.

MARTHA [*pathetic*]: No; no, he is *not* dead; he is not *dead*.

GEORGE: He is dead. Kyrie, eleison. Christe, eleison. Kyrie, eleison.

MARTHA: You *cannot*. You may not decide these things.

NICK [*leaning over her; tenderly*]: He hasn't decided anything, lady. It's not his doing. He doesn't have the power. . . .

GEORGE: That's right, Martha; I'm not a god. I don't have the power over life and death, do I?

MARTHA: YOU CAN'T KILL HIM! YOU CAN'T HAVE HIM DIE!

HONEY: Lady . . . please. . . .

MARTHA: YOU CAN'T!

GEORGE: There was a telegram, Martha.

MARTHA [*up; facing him*]: Show it to me! Show me the telegram!

GEORGE [*long pause; then, with a straight face*]: I ate it.

MARTHA [*a pause; then with the greatest disbelief possible, tinged with hysteria*]: What did you just say to me?

GEORGE [*barely able to stop exploding with laughter*]: I . . . ate . . . it.

[MARTHA *stares at him for a long moment, then spits in his face.*]

GEORGE [*with a smile*]: Good for you, Martha.

NICK [*to* GEORGE]: Do you think that's the way to treat her at a time like this? Making an ugly goddamn joke like that? Hunh?

GEORGE [*snapping his fingers at* HONEY]: Did I eat the telegram or did I not?

HONEY [*terrified*]: Yes; yes, you ate it. I watched . . . I watched you . . . you . . . you ate it all down.

GEORGE [*prompting*]: . . . like a good boy.

HONEY: . . . like a . . . g-g-g-good . . . boy. Yes.

MARTHA [*to* GEORGE, *coldly*]: You're not going to get away with this.

GEORGE [*with disgust*]: YOU KNOW THE RULES, MARTHA! FOR CHRIST'S SAKE, YOU KNOW THE RULES!

MARTHA: NO!

NICK [*with the beginnings of a knowledge he cannot face*]: What are you two talking about?

GEORGE: I can kill him, Martha, if I want to.

MARTHA: HE IS OUR CHILD!

GEORGE: Oh yes, and you bore him, and it was a good delivery. . . .

MARTHA: HE IS OUR CHILD!

GEORGE: AND I HAVE KILLED HIM!

MARTHA: NO!

GEORGE: YES!

 [*Long silence.*]

NICK [*very quietly*]: I think I understand this.

GEORGE [*ibid.*]: Do you?

NICK [*ibid.*]: Jesus Christ, I think I understand this.

GEORGE [*ibid.*]: Good for you, buster.

NICK [*violently*]: JESUS CHRIST I THINK I UNDERSTAND THIS!

MARTHA [*great sadness and loss*]: You have no right. . . you have no right at all. . . .

GEORGE [*tenderly*]: I have the right, Martha. We never spoke of it; that's all. I could kill him any time I wanted to.

MARTHA: But why? Why?

GEORGE: You broke our rule, baby. You mentioned him . . . you mentioned him to someone else.

MARTHA [*tearfully*]: I did *not*. I never did.

GEORGE: Yes, you did.

MARTHA: Who? WHO?!

HONEY [*crying*]: To me. You mentioned him to me.

MARTHA [*crying*]: I FORGET! Sometimes . . . sometimes when it's night, when it's late, and . . . and everybody else is . . . talking . . . I forget and I. . . want to mention him . . . but I . . . HOLD ON . . . I hold on . . . but I've wanted to . . . so often . . . oh, George, you've *pushed* it . . . there was no need . . . there was no need for *this*. I *men*tioned him . . . all right . . . but you didn't have to push it over the EDGE. You didn't have to . . . kill him.

GEORGE: Requiescat in pace.

HONEY: Amen.

MARTHA: You didn't have to have him die, George.

GEORGE: Requiem aeternam dona eis, Domine.

HONEY: Et lux perpetua luceat eis.

MARTHA: That wasn't. . . needed.

[*A long silence.*]

GEORGE [*softly*]: It will be dawn soon. I think the party's over.

NICK [*to* GEORGE; *quietly*]: You couldn't have . . . any?

GEORGE: *We* couldn't.

MARTHA [*a hint of communion in this*]: We couldn't.

GEORGE [*to* NICK *and* HONEY]: Home to bed, children; it's way past your bedtime.

NICK [*his hand out to* HONEY]: Honey?

HONEY [*rising, moving to him*]: Yes.

GEORGE [MARTHA *is sitting on the floor by a chair now*]: You two go now.

NICK: Yes.

HONEY: Yes.

NICK: I'd like to . . .

GEORGE: Good night.

NICK [*pause*]: Good night.

[NICK *and* HONEY *exit;* GEORGE *closes the door after them; looks around the room; sighs, picks up a glass or two, takes them to the bar.*

This whole last section very softly, very slowly.]

GEORGE: Do you want anything, Martha?

MARTHA [*still looking away*]: No . . . nothing.

GEORGE: All right. [*Pause*] Time for bed.

MARTHA: Yes.

GEORGE: Are you tired?

MARTHA: Yes.

GEORGE: I am.

MARTHA: Yes.

GEORGE: Sunday tomorrow; all day.

MARTHA: Yes.

[*A long silence between them.*]

Did you . . . did you . . . have to?

GEORGE [*pause*]: Yes.

MARTHA: It was . . . ? You had to?

GEORGE [*pause*]: Yes.

MARTHA: I don't know.

GEORGE: It was . . . time.

MARTHA: Was it?

GEORGE: Yes.

MARTHA [*pause*]: I'm cold.

GEORGE: It's late.

MARTHA: Yes.

GEORGE [*long silence*]: It will be better.

MARTHA [*long silence*]: I don't. . . know.

GEORGE: It will be . . . maybe.

MARTHA: I'm . . . not. . . sure.

GEORGE: No.

MARTHA: Just . . . us?

GEORGE: Yes.

MARTHA: I don't suppose, maybe, we could . . .

GEORGE: No, Martha.

MARTHA: Yes. No.

GEORGE: Are you all right?

MARTHA: Yes. No.

GEORGE [*puts his hand gently on her shoulder; she puts her head back and he sings to her, very softly*]:
> Who's afraid of Virginia Woolf,
>> Virginia Woolf,
>> Virginia Woolf,

MARTHA: I . . . am . . . George. . . .

GEORGE: Who's afraid of Virginia Woolf. . . .

MARTHA: I . . . am . . . George . . . I . . . am. . . .
> [GEORGE *nods, slowly.*]
> [*Silence; tableau.*]

CURTAIN

penguin.co.uk/vintage

EX LIBRIS

VINTAGE CLASSICS